Praise for *Timebox*

(From real professionals embracing timebox with compassion)

"*I just have to share how much this book resonated with me. I love how Luciana gives readers "permission to balance doing and being." One of the most powerful takeaways from this book is the importance of self-compassion: learning to be kind to ourselves while still pursuing and achieving our goals. It's a message that I think many of us need to hear. Her approach is both insightful and refreshing, making this a must-read for anyone looking to find harmony between ambition and self-care."*
Mariana Maeda - Finance & HR professional

"*In a society where time frequently escapes us like grains of sand, "Timebox" serves as a source of inspiration for those wishing to take charge of their schedules. This book artfully integrates practical techniques, meaningful narratives, and enlightening wisdom, making it a crucial read for anyone eager to improve their efficiency and cultivate a balanced approach to work and life. With this resource, mastering the art of time management is no longer a distant goal, but a realistic possibility, paving the way for a future where time is an empowering ally rather than a hindrance"*.
Luigi Sille - Quality Manager

TIMEBOX

It's Time to Shine

Time Management Strategies to Balance

Productivity and Wellbeing

TIMEBOX, It's Time to Shine
Time management strategies to balance
productivity and wellbeing

Lucy Paulise is a productivity expert, career coach, and award-winning book author dedicated to helping high achievers unlock their full potential. With an MBA, ICF PCC, ASQ CQE, and certifications in Emotional Intelligence (EQ), Trauma-Informed Coaching, and Agile methodologies, she brings over 20 years of experience working with corporations.

Bilingual in English and Spanish, Lucy integrates a deep understanding of emotional resilience, diversity, and self-compassion into her coaching approach. She combines practical strategies with a compassionate and curious mindset to empower professionals to overcome procrastination, perfectionism, and multitasking. She believes that time management isn't about doing more—it's about doing what truly matters with compassion in mind.

Lucy writes for Forbes and is the author of several books, including *We Culture*, *5S Your Life*, and *SOS PYMES*. She received the Phil Crosby Award from ASQ for *We Culture*.

"Reframe your relationship with time—master your day with structure, curiosity, and compassion to shine as your best self."

Luciana (Lucy) Paulise

Timebox, It's Time to Shine: Time Management
Strategies To Balance Productivity And Wellbeing
© 2025 Luciana (Lucy) Paulise
All rights reserved.
Self-Published by:
Biztorming® Training & Consulting LLC
[Spring, Texas, United States]
www.lucypaulise.com

ISBN: 979-8-9987061-2-7
Edition: First Edition
Cover Design by the Author
Interior Formatting by: Luciana Paulise

Disclaimer: This book is for informational and
educational purposes only. The author and publisher make no
representations or warranties concerning the accuracy or
completeness of the contents. The strategies shared should not
be considered professional, medical, or legal advice. Readers
should consult with qualified professionals for personalized
guidance.
Printed in the United States of America
For permissions, inquiries, or bulk purchases, contact
lucy@lucypaulise.com

To Guillermo, Sol and Sofia.
To my mentors and coachees.

Content

Introduction

In a world that constantly demands more of our time and energy, mastering the art of time management has never been more critical. You juggle multiple responsibilities, striving to excel in your career, nurture your relationships, and find time for personal growth. Yet, despite your best efforts, you often end the day feeling overwhelmed, wondering where the hours went. Or maybe you've fallen into the trap of perfectionism, procrastination, or multitasking, only to feel exhausted without the sense of accomplishment you crave. You're not alone—and that's why this book exists.

Executive Brain:
"I know exactly what I need to do—so why can't I just do it?"

Emotional Brain:
"It's not you, it's me."

Exactly. Your emotions get in the way.
I've heard this phrase countless times from professionals, parents, and high achievers alike.

What if you **could** do it? What if you could reclaim your time, reduce stress, and boost productivity—not by relying on sheer willpower but through a system that blends structure with self-compassion?

This isn't just wishful thinking—it's completely achievable.

Welcome to Timebox, It's Time to Shine: Time Management Strategies To Balance Productivity And Wellbeing.

This book isn't just about time management; it's about transforming your relationship with time productively and sustainably, so that you can shine. With the right tools, mindset shifts, and a dose of self-kindness, you'll learn to manage your time purposefully, focus on what truly matters, and move forward—without guilt or burnout.

Why This Book Will Change How You Work

As a career coach, book author, Forbes contributor, and mom of two, I know firsthand the challenge of balancing a packed schedule. Between supporting my clients, writing, and managing my business, I also make time for my husband, cook healthy meals for my family, play tennis, swim, skate, travel, and prioritize quality sleep. It has never been easy; it is a constant struggle. However, through years of experience as a leader, coach, and quality engineer, I've explored countless time management techniques that worked for me and my clients. What I found missing, however, was the key to balance—an approach that ensures productivity without sacrificing joy, health, or self-care.

This book is about helping you refine your time management skills in a way that works for you so you can achieve your goals with efficiency and compassion—without burnout.

You'll discover the transformative power of being intentional about your time management through timeboxing, a proven technique that helps you allocate specific time slots for tasks, ensuring you know what to do throughout your day

and avoiding analysis paralysis. But timeboxing is just the beginning. To truly revolutionize your time management skills, you need to **know what to do first, how to make tasks enjoyable, when to accept that 'good enough' is enough, and when to shut down for your wellbeing.**
This book is not about prescribing a single, rigid solution to time management. Instead, it's a guide to help you explore and experiment with tools and strategies, discovering what works best for your unique personality and lifestyle. Whether you're a perfectionist, a procrastinator, a multitasker or somewhere in between, the insights and practices here are designed to be flexible, empowering you to create a system that aligns with your strengths and addresses your challenges.

Here's what you'll uncover:
Structure for Success:
Timebox: The foundational method for scheduling tasks into focused blocks, helping you map out your day with purpose.

The 3 F's: The "How" to Overcome Common Pitfalls.
- **Focus**: Direct your attention to high-priority tasks, cutting through distractions and honing in on what matters most. Focus addresses prioritization, giving you a clear path through each timebox.
- **Flow**: Get into a rhythm and maintain momentum. Flow counters the urge to avoid challenging tasks and immerses you in work with ease and engagement.
- **Finish**: Embrace progress over perfection. Finish is about closing each task within its allotted timebox, letting go of over-editing, and allowing you to move forward confidently.

Compassion: The Balancing Step.
When pressure builds or burnout threatens, *Compassion* serves as your reset button. This principle

encourages you to pause, recharge, and approach your work with a mindset that values balance, wellbeing, and flexibility.

These principles are theoretical concepts and practical strategies you can implement immediately. Throughout the book, you'll find real-life examples, actionable tips, and interactive exercises designed to help you master these techniques.

What You'll Find in Each Chapter

Every chapter is structured to provide you with a comprehensive, actionable toolkit for transformation. Here's what you can expect:

1. **Quotes from Real People:**
    Relatable insights and stories from individuals who have faced the same struggles show you that you're not alone and that change is possible.
2. **Common Challenges:**
    A breakdown of the specific issues that hold you back, helping you identify the root causes of your struggles with time and focus.
3. **Reflection Questions:**
    After exploring these challenges, you'll find thought-provoking questions to help you reflect on your own habits and experiences. These questions are designed to increase self-awareness and prepare you to apply the solutions effectively.
4. **Benefits of the Proposed Solutions:**
    Why these strategies work, backed by science, research, and practical examples, so you can see how they lead to real results.
5. **Behavioral Shifts to Achieve [Focus/Flow/Finishing]:**

Practical adjustments you can make to your habits and routines that align your actions with your goals.

6. **Emotional Regulation Shifts:**
   Insights on how to leverage emotional intelligence and self-compassion to overcome mental roadblocks and maintain your motivation.

7. **Practical Tips to Implement Now:**
   You can take immediate action today to start seeing results because progress shouldn't have to wait.

8. **Takeaways to Remember:**
   Key points are summarized at the end of each chapter to reinforce the most important lessons and help you apply them consistently.

Why This Approach Works

This structure ensures you are not just reading about time management, you are actively learning, reflecting, and implementing as you go. Integrating behavioral and emotional shifts with practical tips gives you a balanced approach to creating sustainable change. Whether you're a procrastinator, a multitasker, or a perfectionist, this book is your step-by-step guide to reclaiming your time and life.

It's time to shine. Let's get started.

Want Extra Support as You Read?

If you love applying what you learn right away (or just like a little structure), I've got you covered.

To complement this book, I've created a set of free companion resources to help you take action and stay on track:

- **The Time Management Personality Quiz** – Discover your unique time style so you can personalize your plan

- **The Timebox On-Demand Course** – Master the method with self-paced videos, examples, and templates

- **Downloadable Worksheets and Checklists** – Print-friendly tools to support your daily timeboxing practice

- **1-on-1 Coaching Sessions** – If you want personalized guidance, book a coaching session to move forward with clarity and confidence.

You can access everything at:

www.lucypaulise.com/timebox

Feel free to check it out now—or come back to it whenever you're ready to dive deeper.

It's time to shine. Let's get started.

Chapter 1 | It's Time
The Two Sides of Time Management

"Time management is a balancing act between what you want to do and what you should do."

"I woke up early today, ready to dive into writing. I planned to start working at 7:00, an hour earlier than usual, to catch up. I had breakfast, organized my day, and then sat down to write at 7:04. At 7:05—and I am not exaggerating, it was exactly one minute later—my daughter woke up and started crying, needing my attention. My husband was out running, so I had to step in. Suddenly, the time I had carved out for focus disappeared."

You can plan every detail, but then reality strikes. Those moments, which could have led to frustration and self-criticism, instead taught me the value of managing my time with compassion—not just for others, but for myself. I learned that plans were necessary so I could use them wisely whenever I had a minute. While I couldn't write, I could at least jot down some thoughts, reprioritize my calendar, or reach out to my ChatGPT to refine some ideas. I had to accept what was possible, prioritize by urgency, and plan with buffers in my day. Compassion became my lifeline, helping me navigate interruptions with grace instead of guilt and, ultimately, to finish this book.

This is not just my story—it's a reality many face in a world filled with competing demands. Whether it's work deadlines, family responsibilities, or personal goals, the chaos of life often feels unmanageable. For high performers, this can lead to cycles of frustration, burnout, and a constant sense of falling short.

Effective time management is essential for achieving work-life balance. Some people are perfectionists by nature, spending hours on a single task or overworking; others procrastinate, often waiting until the last minute to complete tasks or routinely missing deadlines. Meanwhile, a few people manage to accomplish more in less time, feeling happier, less stressed, and more satisfied with their achievements. What sets them apart?

What sets them apart is that they know what matters most is how you feel about your day, not just what you did. It's not just about checking off tasks—it's about whether you feel accomplished, frustrated, overwhelmed, or a mix of everything when you close your computer or wrap up with your last client. In my coaching sessions, I've seen how many people struggle with time management. The growing number of daily meetings, tasks, and emails can be overwhelming, making it harder to focus on what really matters.

From reducing emails and meeting time to prioritizing tasks and learning to say no, I've developed a variety of tools to help people become more productive and content.

In this book, we'll explore how practical time management strategies, combined with self-compassion, can help you achieve more and feel more at peace while doing so. From focusing on what matters most to embracing the inevitable interruptions, this journey will help you reframe your approach to time and redefine success.

Compassion is often misunderstood as a luxury or weakness, but in truth, it's a powerful tool for resilience and productivity. It's not about lowering standards or giving up on ambition. Compassion is about recognizing our limits, adjusting expectations, and continuing forward with grace. The key to integrating more compassion into your time management is this: when you feel frustrated, you take action to address it rather than suffering in silence or risking burnout.

To end each day feeling truly satisfied, you need to master your time and priorities with compassion rather than letting tasks take over. Achieving this requires consistently applying specific behaviors throughout the day.

The Brain's Executive Function

Is time management more challenging for some people than others? Absolutely. Time management is intricately linked to our executive function—the cognitive processes that enable us to plan, focus, and follow through on tasks. For individuals with ADHD (Attention Deficit Hyperactivity Disorder), for example, challenges with executive function can make these steps feel daunting, often leading to difficulties in maintaining focus, achieving flow, and completing tasks. This book offers practical tools to strengthen these essential skills, helping everyone, including those with ADHD, manage time with greater ease and confidence.

The Other side of Time Management

But surprisingly, time management isn't just about exercising the executive function of the brain, mastering tools, adopting habits, or even training your brain's executive function to get more done. While these strategies are helpful, they're only part of the equation.

Have you ever had a day where everything is planned perfectly, yet you still feel stuck or overwhelmed? Let's say you have a big project due. Instead of diving into it, you find yourself cleaning your desk or scrolling through social media. On the surface, it looks like procrastination. But underneath, your self-talk might be saying, *"This project is too hard. What if I fail?"* This emotional undercurrent not only delays the work but also depletes your energy and confidence.

This isn't a failure of strategy—it's an emotional barrier. Negative self-talk, fear of failure, imposter syndrome, or perfectionism often creep into our subconscious, turning us into our own worst enemies.

These hidden narratives create resistance and make even simple tasks feel overwhelming. They're not just time-wasters—they're energy-drainers that keep you from achieving your full potential.

This is connected to the amygdala, the part of the brain responsible for processing emotions, which operates in opposition to the prefrontal cortex—the area of the brain involved in executive function. When the amygdala is activated by fear or stress, it can hijack our ability to think clearly, focus, and follow through, making emotional barriers even harder to overcome. Understanding this dynamic is key to unlocking your potential and managing both the emotional and practical sides of time management.

Real, sustainable time management is about finding balance within.

Balance is the key to aligning your intentions and expectations with your external actions and your internal emotions. It's the art of navigating your tasks while managing the feelings and self-talk that can either propel you forward or hold you back. When we overlook this emotional side of time management, we risk creating a cycle of overwork, self-criticism, and burnout.

Achieving balance means:
- Recognizing when to push and when to pause.
- Giving yourself permission to rest without guilt.
- Aligning your tasks with your values and energy levels.

Compassion: The Key to Balance

How do you achieve balance? Compassion is the foundation of balance. When we let self-criticism dominate, balance becomes impossible. Compassion allows us to pause, reflect, and reset without judgment. Instead of focusing on what you didn't accomplish, compassion invites you to celebrate what you did achieve, understand what happened and learn from it.

For example:
- If you fall behind on a task, replace "I'm so disorganized" with "I did my best with the time I had. What can I learn to improve next time?"
- If you feel overwhelmed, ask yourself, "What's one thing I can let go of to restore balance?"
  Balancing Doing and Being
  True balance is about mastering the dance between *doing* and *being*. Some days will be about tackling your biggest priorities; others will be about slowing down to recharge. Balance means recognizing that rest is as valuable as action and that productivity thrives when paired with self-care.

Time management is more than just tips and tools; it's about creating harmony between external tasks and internal emotions. By embracing balance and managing your self-talk, you can turn time management from a battle against the clock into a partnership with yourself. It's not just about managing your time—it's about creating a meaningful, fulfilling, and sustainable life so you can shine.

In the following chapters, we'll explore how strategies like timeboxing can help you compartmentalize different areas of your life, allowing you to focus fully on the task at hand and achieve the balance you need to thrive in all aspects of your life.

Chapter 2 | CHALLENGES

What is Wrong with Your Current Time Management System?

"I feel like I'm constantly busy but never actually accomplishing what matters. My to-do list grows faster than I can check things off, and at the end of the day, I'm exhausted and frustrated, wondering where all my time went."

Many say being busy isn't the same as being effective, right? You may be doing a lot, but you feel like you've accomplished nothing at the end of the day. This common struggle often arises from poor prioritization and spending too much time on the wrong activities. Decisions in the heat of the moment, distractions, and unexpected tasks can derail your focus and productivity.

Effective time management is crucial for productivity and success, yet many people struggle to find a system that truly works for them. If you often feel overwhelmed by tasks or constantly run out of time, it might be time to re-evaluate your approach.

Traditional time management systems, like to-do lists, often fail to address the root causes of disorganization and lack of productivity. While to-do lists work for some people, depending on their personality and temperament, they can quickly become a source of stress for others.

What About My To-do List?

While these lists help prioritize tasks, they also highlight the overwhelming burden of multiple responsibilities, which can be frustrating at the end of the day. They normally don't have a structure, as it is just a list of things to get done, so without a clear structure, it's easy to get sidetracked or overwhelmed. If task complexity and priorities are not analyzed, some tasks could take hours while others could be two-minute tasks; some can be urgent and some not.

To-do lists usually don't tell you how long to spend on a task or when to do it, and they tend to overwhelm you by showing how many tasks you still have pending. In essence, they tend to be unrealistic.

Traditional paper to-do lists can be limiting since tasks cannot be rearranged or prioritized easily. Online to-do lists like Google Tasks can solve some of these issues as you can rearrange and set due dates and reminders. Still, both online and paper to-do lists share a common pitfall, which is their tendency to become overwhelming[i]. With an ever-growing list of tasks that can leave us feeling anxious and paralyzed. Additionally, without proper prioritization, you often jump from one task to another without a clear focus, leading to reduced productivity and quality of work.

To-do lists often have an inherent flaw: they encourage the user to be overly ambitious and overcommit. The busier you are, the more you overestimate your capabilities and underestimate the time required to complete tasks. This leads to constant disappointment and stress when your to-do list shows only 2 out of 10 "Done" items at the end of the day.

Some tasks seem too big and complex, and you don't want to start working on them. Some others are so simple that adding them to your to-do list takes longer than doing them. But if you actually count them, they build up into so many items that they seem impossible and overwhelming. In the end, either because they are too complex or too simple, you never start working on them or spend too much on unnecessary details. Blame Parkinson's Law for this phenomenon.

Parkinson's Law

British historian and author Cyril Northcote Parkinson formulated *Parkinson's Law*: "Work expands to fill the time available for its completion." If you give yourself three weeks to complete a task, you might unconsciously stretch it to fill the entire time frame—even if you could realistically finish it much sooner. A typical example of this is in meetings. When meetings are scheduled for one hour, you may notice that they always take the entire hour. How is this possible? Is it due to flawless planning? Not necessarily—it's Parkinson's Law in action. If you plan a meeting, you may unintentionally expand the scope of the discussion or adjust the pace to ensure the meeting lasts the full allotted time. We tend to value our commitments and agreements, but what if moving forward, you placed more value on finishing a meeting early for the sake of our wellbeing?

Instead, you could use Parkinson's Law to your advantage by planning small, focused time blocks for similar tasks, creating a sense of urgency to complete them within a more compact time frame. By doing this, you can increase productivity, reduce procrastination, and prevent tasks from unnecessarily ballooning into time-consuming activities. Instead of stretching tasks to fill available time, you will complete them with greater efficiency and enjoy more free time.

Last but not least, traditional to-do lists often neglect the most crucial aspect of our pursuit of productivity and achievement: our wellbeing. You normally would not add to your to-do list your time for exercise, breaks, social connections, and hobbies.

While to-do lists are invaluable tools for managing our careers and personal lives, they are not immune to shortcomings. By recognizing their limitations, you can balance accomplishing tasks and nurturing your wellbeing, achieving greater satisfaction and success in your professional endeavors.

The 5 P's of Time Management Issues

The main issues often boil down to what I call the *5 P's* of time management challenges: planning, procrastination, perfectionism, prioritization, and passion. Let's break down what might be wrong with your current time management system and how timeboxing can help.

1. **Planning**
    "If you don't plan, you plan to fail," as the saying goes. Spending time up front to clarify what's most important can be game-changing. However, many people skip planning because they're "too busy," while others over-plan to the point that they never get started. Finding the right balance between thoughtful planning and taking action is essential.

2. **Prioritization**
    Many people need help with prioritization, often focusing on less impactful tasks at the expense of more critical ones. This can lead to spending too much time

on activities that don't contribute meaningfully to your goals. Learning to differentiate between high-impact tasks and "busywork" is crucial for effective time management.

3. **Procrastination**
Procrastination is one of the most common barriers to effective time management. Delaying tasks can lead to last-minute stress, rushed work, and lower-quality results. It often stems from fear of failure, lack of motivation, or feeling overwhelmed by complex tasks. Identifying why you procrastinate can help break the cycle.

4. **Perfectionism**
While striving for excellence is commendable, perfectionism can be paralyzing. It often causes people to spend excessive time on minor details, preventing them from moving on to other important tasks. Perfectionists may also delay starting tasks out of fear they won't meet their high standards. The key is to recognize that "done for now" is sometimes better than "perfect."

5. **Passion**
Passion can be a double-edged sword. While it fuels productivity, it can also lead to overcommitment. Being overly enthusiastic about multiple projects can spread you thin, diminishing your effectiveness and increasing the risk of burnout. Balancing passion with realistic limits helps you stay focused and work at a sustainable pace.

Unfortunately, a lot of the frustrations we experience with time management are simply created by our minds. Yes, external demands from clients and managers, continuous emails and Slack messages are totally real, and pushing yourself to accomplish something is not so terrible. But trying to make it all perfect and faster than anyone won't help you in the long term.

What happens is that we are all, at all times, having an internal conversation with ourselves. Should I do this, or should I do that? Should I sleep more, or should I finish my work? Should I do exercise or watch that new episode? At least, we have two of ourselves. One "self" that is very, very demanding, like an 8-year-old asking for attention.

This self is driven by external expectations, deadlines, and the desire to accomplish as much as possible, often pushing us to go above and beyond, sometimes at the expense of our health and happiness. It has a relentless need for approval, and the fear of not measuring up makes it hard to rest.

Then, there is the other self—the quieter, more nurturing voice that is attuned to your wellbeing. It knows when you're tired, when you need a break, and when you need to take care of your mental and emotional health. This self is compassionate and values long-term health and sustainability over short-term accomplishments. It may not always be as loud as the demanding self, but it's crucial for helping you create balance. Do you ever listen to it? When you do, you can make better decisions that align with both your goals and your wellbeing.

Your brain may say yes to the goal and commitment, but your wellbeing says no. Here is where the struggle starts.

Coping Mechanisms

Whenever we perceive a struggle, frustration or unmet need, our brain interprets it as a threat. In response, we may instinctively react in one of three ways: **fight**, **flight**, or **freeze**. These are unconscious coping mechanisms that manifest as **overcompensation** (fight), **avoidance** (flight), or **surrender** (freeze).

For example, you might view the situation as threatening when overwhelmed by too many tasks. This can lead to perfectionism—working late into the night obsessing on the details (overcompensation), procrastination—delaying the work altogether (avoidance), or surrender—feeling defeated or like a failure and not knowing where to start (surrender).

In this book, we'll explore how these biological stress responses often shape our time management habits. Whether you're overcommitting, procrastinating, or feeling stuck, I'll guide you through the **focus**, **flow**, and **finish** approach to break free from these instinctive reactions and regain control of your time.

Achieving Balance

By understanding these natural responses (freeze, flight, fight), being aware when you are about to experience them and exploring other ways to react with focus, flow, and finish strategies, you can talk yourself out of it to be able to manage your time more effectively, reduce stress and do more of what you love. The key is to recognize the triggers that push you into survival mode, identify your typical response mode, and apply the right time management strategy and compassion to regain control and respond differently.

Self-compassion As a Balancer

My time management approach combines proven practical tools with the power of self-compassion, aligning strategies with your natural responses. It's about treating yourself with kindness and understanding, especially during moments of struggle or setbacks. Instead of falling into the trap of self-criticism, this approach helps you sustain your passion without the weight of perfectionism or fear of failure. When you practice self-compassion, you build resilience, allowing you to recover from challenges more effectively—so you can stay motivated, focused, and committed to your goals without burning out.

By striking the right balance, you can learn to trust your decision-making to start, understand what motivates you so that you can engage in various tasks and regulate your attention to detail so that you can get things done.

Each time management challenge can be effectively addressed by applying the five core principles of the book: timeboxing, focus, flow, finish, and compassion. These principles offer practical solutions to common time management issues and foster a balanced approach to productivity and wellbeing.

Here's how each principle connects to specific time management issues and provides a practical solution before, during and after completing a task:

BEFORE
1. **Planning → Timeboxing**
    Planning is essential, but it can easily veer into either over-preparation or avoidance. *Timeboxing* provides a structured approach, setting clear time limits for tasks, which helps prevent the pitfalls of over-planning. By confining each task to a specific block of time, you prioritize action over exhaustive preparation, ensuring a steady flow through your workday.

DURING: The 3 F's
2.   **Prioritization → Focus**
    Knowing where to start. Poor prioritization can lead to scattered attention, often focusing on lower-impact tasks while neglecting high-priority ones. The

principle of *Focus* encourages you to fully engage with one task at a time, spotlighting what truly matters. This way, you avoid the trap of multitasking and ensure your energy goes toward meaningful work.

3.   **Procrastination → Flow**
Knowing how long to stay on a task.
Procrastination often stems from avoidance or feeling overwhelmed by a task's complexity and, hence, not being able to sustain attention on it. The principle of *flow* helps you overcome this by encouraging immersion in each task and connecting it to a meaningful purpose. You can create a rhythm that makes it easier to dive in, perform, and gain momentum, reducing the tendency to put things off.

4.   **Perfectionism → Finish**
Knowing when to stop the task. Perfectionism can lead to endless tweaking, delaying completion. *Finish* emphasizes the importance of getting tasks done within the set time, focusing on "progress for now" rather than perfection. By adhering to a time limit, you push past the need for flawless execution and embrace the satisfaction of completion, moving steadily forward.

AFTER: Compassion, The Balancing Step
5.   **Passion → Following up with Compassion**
Passion can drive productivity, but it may also lead to overcommitment and burnout. The principle of *Compassion* reminds you to respect your own limits by loving yourself before anything or anybody else, ensuring sustainable productivity. By honoring your need for balance, you channel your passion constructively without overwhelming yourself, maintaining both motivation and wellbeing.

Question for you
What is your typical response mode under stress?

What's next

In the next chapter, you will gain deeper insights into your typical time management mode, allowing you to prioritize the techniques that best align with your approach.

Chapter 3 | TIME MANAGEMENT QUIZ

What Is Your Time Management Style?

How Your Time Management Style Shapes Your Productivity

"I always thought I was great at multitasking until things got hectic. Under stress, my productivity plummets, and I end up spinning my wheels without getting anything done. I wish I could find a better way to manage my time when it really counts."

Have you ever wondered why some people breeze through their tasks while others struggle to keep up? Everyone approaches time management differently, shaped by their habits, personalities, and experiences. By understanding your natural time management mode, you can identify strengths to leverage and weaknesses to address, helping you create a system that works best for you.

I've developed a simple time management quiz to simplify this process. I understand that reading the entire book might feel overwhelming and time-consuming. This personality assessment will help you identify your default way of managing time, traits and tendencies, so you can prioritize which chapters to focus on first. Whether you need to tackle perfectionism, decision fatigue, or setting boundaries, this tool allows you to customize your learning experience so you can start with the areas that will provide the most significant benefit the fastest, based on your unique personality.

It's designed to help you discover your default mode when managing tasks and deadlines, whether in control or under stress. Once you've identified your mode, you'll gain personalized insights and strategies to improve.

As a coach, I aim to guide you by sharing tools and strategies that have helped many others. However, time management is not a one-size-fits-all approach. What works best for you will depend on your unique style, preferences, and circumstances. I encourage you to experiment, mix and match the tools in this book, and adapt them to fit your life.

Your typical response mode may also shift depending on the situation. If that happens, exploring the other modes will help you develop a well-rounded approach, ensuring you're prepared to manage your time effectively in any scenario.

How to Calculate Your Time Management Style:

To calculate your **primary time management mode**, follow these steps:

1. Answer each question in the assessment by selecting the option (A, B, C, or D) that best describes your typical behavior.
2. Record your answers in the table provided, marking A, B, C, or D for each question.
3. Tally your responses: Count how many times you selected each letter (A, B, C, or D).

4. Determine your primary mode: The category with the most responses represents your dominant time management mode.

5. Analyze your results:
   - If one mode is significantly higher than the others, that is your primary time management style.
   - If you have a mix of responses, you may exhibit characteristics of multiple modes, meaning your approach shifts based on different situations, and you show a situational mode.

You can also take the test online at

https://www.lucypaulise.com/timebox/

1. **How do you usually start your workday**
   A) I start with a clear plan but often get distracted by emails or other tasks.
   B) I struggle to get going and procrastinate on tasks I don't enjoy.
   C) I dive in but spend too much time perfecting one task.
   D) I start with a prioritized plan and stay focused on the most important tasks.

2. **What is your reaction when faced with a long to-do list?**
   A) I try to juggle multiple things at once, often losing track of priorities.
   B) I put off starting, especially on tasks I find boring or irrelevant.
   C) I overcommit and stress over getting everything done perfectly.
   D) I prioritize tasks by importance and tackle them one at a time.

3. **How do you typically respond to deadlines?**
   A) I often switch between tasks and lose focus, leaving things until the last minute.
   B) I avoid them until they're too close, then rush.
   C) I meticulously plan but frequently underestimate how long things will take.
   D) I set realistic milestones and pace myself to meet the deadline.

4. **What's your biggest challenge with managing your time?**
   A) I get easily distracted by new tasks or notifications.
   B) I procrastinate on tasks that don't excite me.
   C) I tend to overwork to make sure things are perfect.

D) I balance focus and flexibility, prioritizing tasks effectively.

5. When you complete a task, how do you feel?

A) I feel scattered and often have to go back to unfinished items.

B) I'm relieved but feel like I could've done better if I started earlier.

C) I worry it's not good enough and sometimes rework it even after it's done.

D) I feel accomplished, knowing I gave it my best effort.

6. How do you handle unexpected tasks that come up during your workday?

A) I immediately switch to the new task, leaving others incomplete.

B) I avoid dealing with it, hoping it resolves itself or someone else handles it.

C) I feel overwhelmed and try to handle it perfectly, sometimes delaying other tasks.

D) I assess its importance, prioritize it, and adjust my schedule as needed.

7. What is your approach to planning your week?

A) I create a plan but get sidetracked by unplanned events or tasks.

B) I delay planning and only react to what feels urgent.

C) I over-plan every detail, often spending more time planning than doing.

D) I outline key priorities and leave room for flexibility.

8. How do you respond when your work is interrupted?

A) I quickly switch to the interruption and forget what I was doing.

B) I might delay addressing the interruption or avoid it, causing me to mentally dwell on it instead of refocusing on my original task.

C) I feel guilty if I don't respond to the interruption, but then I feel frustrated because I have less time to finish what I was doing.

D) I acknowledge the interruption and decide if it requires immediate attention or if I can wait.

9. When you're assigned a new project, how do you approach it?

A) I dive into multiple parts at once, often losing track of priorities.

B) I delay starting until it becomes urgent.

C) I focus excessively on perfecting the initial stages, often getting caught in details, which causes delays and leaves me with less time to complete the later stages of the project, creating unnecessary pressure.

D) I break it into smaller steps and set realistic milestones.

10. At the end of the day, how do you feel about your accomplishments?

A) I feel scattered, as I've started many things but finished a few.

B) I feel disappointed for not starting tasks I avoided.

C) I feel drained because I worked too hard to make everything perfect.

D) I feel satisfied, knowing I focused on the most important tasks.

Questions	A	B	C	D
1. How do you usually start your workday?				
2. What is your reaction when faced with a long to-do list?				
3. How do you typically respond to deadlines?				
4. What's your biggest challenge with managing your time?				
5. When you complete a task, how do you feel?				
6. How do you handle unexpected tasks that come up during your workday?				
7. What is your approach to planning your week?				
8. How do you respond when your work is interrupted?				
9. When you're assigned a new project, how do you approach it?				
10. At the end of the day, how do you feel about your accomplishments?				

TOTAL SCORE				

Time Management Assessment: Understanding Your Primary Mode

Your responses in this assessment reveal your dominant time management style. The category with the most responses represents your primary time management mode.

A: Multitasker
B: Procrastinator
C: Perfectionist
D: Balanced

If two or more categories are tied, you may have a **situational mode**, meaning your time management tendencies shift based on different situations.

You can review the recommendations for your dominant mode by going directly to that chapter and experimenting with strategies to improve your productivity and balance.

Below are descriptions of each category:

A: The Multitasker

You thrive in fast-paced environments and often juggle multiple tasks at once. While this may give you a sense of productivity, frequent task-switching can reduce efficiency and increase stress. You may find it challenging to focus deeply on one task at a time, leading to incomplete work or mental fatigue. Implementing timeboxing and single-tasking strategies can help you improve focus and effectiveness. Go to Chapter 5 to learn more.

B: The Procrastinator

You tend to put off tasks, especially those that seem difficult or uninteresting. While you may work well under pressure, relying on urgency often leads to stress and last-minute scrambling. You might struggle with getting started or staying motivated. Breaking tasks into smaller steps, setting clear deadlines, and understanding your motivations can help you overcome procrastination and build momentum. Go to Chapter 6 to learn more.

C: The Perfectionist

You set high standards and strive for flawless execution. While this ensures quality, it can also slow you down, leading to overanalysis, hesitation, or fear of failure. You may struggle with knowing when a task is "good enough" to move on. Learning to define realistic completion points and embracing progress over perfection will help you become more efficient while maintaining high standards. Go to Chapter 7 to learn more.

D: The Balanced Time Manager

You manage your time effectively while maintaining a healthy balance between productivity and wellbeing. Unlike the other styles, you don't fall into extremes of multitasking, procrastination, or perfectionism. You prioritize tasks strategically, set realistic goals, and allow time for rest and personal wellbeing. Your approach allows for high performance and sustainable success, making you adaptable and resilient. Continuous reflection and minor adjustments help you maintain this balance over time. Read more about the other modes to understand how your coworkers think and feel.

By discovering your time management mode, you'll gain insights into your natural tendencies and common behaviors, helping you focus on the tools that align with your strengths and address your challenges. Now, explore all the chapters to gain a broader perspective on different approaches, understand your team members' preferred mode of work, or focus by heading to the chapter that best aligns with your primary time management mode.

Chapter 4 | TIMEBOX
Planning What to Do

How to structure your day with timeboxing to set your day for success.

"I try to plan my day, but by the time I open my inbox in the morning, there are already 20 new emails demanding my attention. With nearly 100 emails coming in daily, my priorities constantly shift. How can I ever stick to a plan or make meaningful progress?"

I have vivid memories of my time in corporate America nearly two decades ago, at the height of the BlackBerry era. It was challenging to stay focused on my tasks and meet deadlines while juggling multiple team meetings, one-on-one planning sessions, and stress management. Although I was thrilled to lead a team, I struggled to set boundaries with upper management, peers, direct reports, and other teams. Direct reports would show up at my desk, my manager would pull me into meetings, and colleagues would email me with urgent requests. I eagerly participated in everything and never thought about declining an opportunity.

At that time, working on-site with an open-door policy was standard, making it nearly impossible to have uninterrupted time for myself. However, I soon realized that to enjoy my work and maintain productivity, I needed to prioritize "me" time. My calendar became my primary tool to navigate this demanding environment. I started blocking specific times each day to focus on certain tasks and avoid random meeting bookings. Some coworkers were surprised to see my calendar filled with "invisible" meetings, thinking it was neither fair nor genuine. But I saw this as essential busy time—time just as valuable as any meeting.

Several years later, I transitioned to independent consulting and coaching. During my study of agile methods and Kanban, I recognized that what I had been practicing was "timeboxing."

What Is Timeboxing?

Timeboxing is a productivity system where you intentionally block time on your calendar in advance to do the tasks that are more important to you. Timeboxing helps you decide what to do, when, and for how long. Unlike a traditional to-do list, which often grows endlessly, timeboxing ensures that each task has a defined slot on your calendar with a specific start and end time. It encourages mindful scheduling, helping you manage your workload and set realistic expectations.

By blocking time for specific tasks, you can:
- Avoid overcommitting.
- Communicate priorities and boundaries clearly to others.

- Evaluate how you spend your time and adjust as needed.
- Reduce distractions and analysis paralysis by having a pre-decided plan.
- Allocate specific time slots for each task on your to-do list, ensuring that you complete the work within the designated time following Parkinson's law.

Timeboxing goes beyond just planning your day—it also helps you reflect. At the end of the day, you can assess your schedule, understand your productivity patterns, and celebrate your accomplishments.

Steps to Start Timeboxing

Choose a System or App

To start timeboxing, decide how you'll schedule your tasks. You can use your digital or paper calendar, such as Google Calendar, Outlook, or Apple Calendar, or explore tools like Sunsama[ii], Jira, or Trello to track tasks efficiently, including their timing and duration. Choose the tool that fits your workflow and helps you stay organized while visualizing your time. You'll find more in the Recommended Tools addendum at the end of the book.

Turn Your To-Do List Into a Backlog

A backlog, popularized by agile methodologies like Scrum, is a dynamic list of all potential tasks—short-term, long-term, realistic, or even aspirational. Think of it as a central repository feeding your daily timeboxing. By keeping a digital backlog, you can easily reprioritize as needs change. Integrate it with your calendar so that when it's time to plan your day, you can quickly pick the most urgent and important tasks. This approach also allows you to break larger tasks into smaller, more manageable parts that fit neatly into your schedule.

It's recommended that you have a digital backlog instead of using Post-it or handwritten notes since it's easier to move tasks around based on changing priorities. If you already have an online to-do list, you can look for ways to integrate it with your calendar and your backlog to make it easier to implement.

Consolidate your calendar events, meetings, emails, tasks, paper todo-lists and post-it notes into one unified to-do list or backlog. Multiple tools and systems often lead to underestimation of your workload. Align all these sources into one place for better clarity and prioritization.

Your backlog might differ from your team's system, creating confusion. In this case, if you can also use the same time management system that your team members use, that would be a huge communication tool.

Prioritize tasks by bringing the most important and urgent ones to the top of your list while deferring non-urgent or "desired" tasks. The order will emphasize due dates and priorities.

Define a Timeframe

Next, define your **timeframe**, also known as a sprint. This could span a day, a week, or a month, the typical period of time or frequency that you will set a timeboxing routine.

My recommendation is to timebox one day at a time. You can do weekly planning if your schedule doesn't normally change much. Be realistic about what you can accomplish by scheduling the most important tasks first and making sure they all fit into your calendar. I normally only timebox fixed events or meetings with other people, and I timebox my tasks day by day as a reminder of how my day should go.

Set a Template

Timeboxing day by day doesn't mean that you start every day from scratch. Just like you may have regular meetings scheduled in advance, schedule your own events and tasks as if you had a template. You can schedule blocks to be repeated weekly, daily or even monthly, like gym classes, kids' pick-up, writing time, or time to reach out to clients so that half of your work is already done, and you can only add unique events to your calendar.

Behavioral Shifts to Maximize Timeboxing

It's Time to Timebox Your Calendar

Now that you know what you need to do first, start timeboxing—scheduling every key task on your calendar (see Image below) to take advantage of Parkinson's Law and protect your precious time.

You can block time on your calendar for focus work in different ways depending on how you want to manage interruptions. You can mark the time as **busy**, which signals to others that you're unavailable during that period, or you can block it off and keep it marked as **free**, so it's strictly reserved for you, while still allowing others to send invitations if needed. Treat these time blocks like appointments with yourself—just as you would schedule a one-hour meeting, do the same for your "focus time" on critical tasks. This allows you to create a dedicated space for productivity without feeling pressured by others' demands. Planning one day at a time helps keep you flexible and realistic. Start by blocking off non-negotiable events (meetings, deadlines, or any "template" tasks you've already defined), then fill in the rest of your day with tasks from your backlog.

8:00 AM - 8:45 AM: Write article (Focus Time)

8:45 AM - 9:00 AM: Buffer time and quick break

9:00 AM - 11:00 AM: Tennis classes (Personal time for workout and shower)

11:00 AM - 11:45 AM: Coaching Session with Client (High-priority work)

11:45 AM - 12:00 PM: Buffer time and quick break

12:00 PM - 1:00 PM: Lunch Break (Rest and recharge)

1:00 PM - 1:45 PM: Coaching Session with Client (High-priority work)

1:45 AM - 2:00 PM: Buffer time and quick break

2:00 PM - 2:45 PM: LinkedIn Post and Newsletter (Administrative Tasks like Emails, follow-up on action items)

2:45 AM - 3:00 PM: Buffer time and quick break

3:00 PM - 3:30 PM: Learning and Creativity time

3:30 PM - 4:00 PM: Pick up Sol

4:00 PM - 5:45 PM: Availability for new clients

5:45 PM - 6:00 PM: Daily Shutdown (End of day review, prepare for tomorrow)

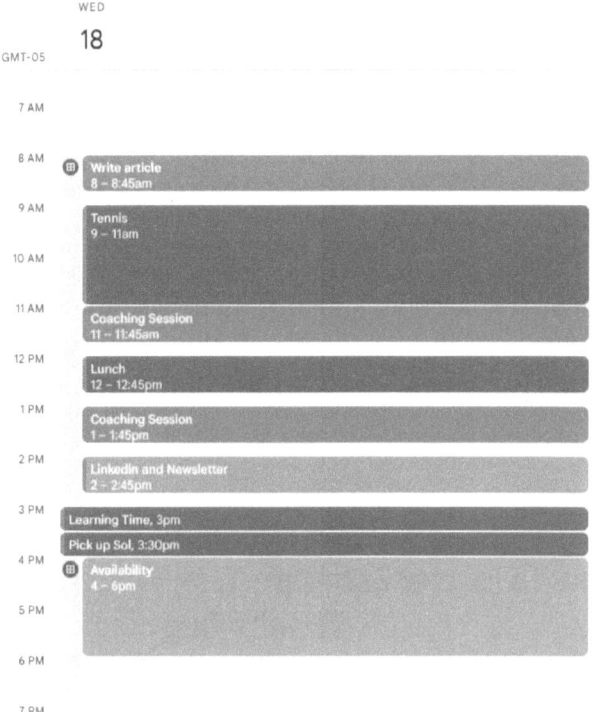

You may have heard of time blocking, which involves marking time on your calendar as "busy" to prevent interruptions, but Timeboxing goes a step further. A timebox is a fixed duration dedicated to a specific task or activity, with the goal of accomplishing as much as possible within that time frame. Once the time is up, stop working on the task, regardless of its completion. The focus is on productivity within a set time limit, not on perfection or finishing everything.

Ensure that each timeboxed task is scheduled with a clear title, purpose, duration, and definition of done (more on this in the Finish chapter).

Being specific when describing a task is crucial for reducing overwhelm and improving efficiency. Vague tasks like "work on a presentation" or "write a report" can feel daunting because they lack clear starting points and measurable progress. Instead, breaking them down into actionable steps— such as "outline key points for presentation" or "draft the introduction section of the report"—helps you understand exactly what needs to be done. This clarity makes it easier to estimate the time required and prevents procrastination caused by uncertainty.

When you define tasks with precision, you create a roadmap for execution, making them feel more manageable and increasing the likelihood of getting them done.

Now, go to your backlog and fill your day with important tasks first.

How to Better Estimate Task Time for Effective Timeboxing

Accurately estimating how long a task will take is essential for successful timeboxing. Underestimating can lead to frustration and rushed work, while overestimating can result in wasted time. Here are some strategies to improve your time estimation skills:

- Instead of estimating a large, vague task, break it down into smaller, more specific actions. This makes assessing the time required for each step easier and reduces the risk of underestimating.

- Use the *Past as a Guide*. Reflect on similar tasks you've completed before. How long did they take? If you tend to underestimate, add a buffer of 20-30% more time than your initial guess.
- Track Your Work. Keep a log of how long different types of tasks take. Over time, you'll notice patterns and improve your ability to estimate accurately.
- Test and Adjust – Set a time limit and work on the task until the timer runs out. Take note of how much you accomplished and adjust your future estimates accordingly.

By fine-tuning your ability to estimate time realistically, you'll make timeboxing more effective, ensuring you have enough time to focus on tasks without feeling overwhelmed or running behind schedule.

Create a Routine

Routines are vital for productivity and mental health, yet creatives, innovators, and freelancers often overlook them. Establishing a simple "planning routine" helps reduce stress, improve focus, and create a sense of order.

Dedicate 15 minutes at the start or end of your workday to plan. If you're a morning person, plan the day ahead as part of your morning routine. Not a fan of early mornings? Plan the night before so you can jump straight into action the next day. Planning daily, rather than far in advance, allows for more accurate prioritization and flexibility.

A morning planning routine sets the tone for a productive day, enabling you to tackle your most important tasks before distractions arise. For evening planners, ending the day with a clear plan offers the same sense of control and helps you unwind, reducing stress for the next day.

Remember: skipping planning is risky—without it, you're essentially planning to fail. Whether you prefer mornings or evenings, incorporate this routine into your schedule to start achieving more with less stress.

Now, it's time to fit the most important tasks into your calendar, setting yourself up for a productive day.

During your 15-minute daily planning session, start by assessing your actual availability. It's easy to overestimate what you can accomplish and overload your schedule, leading to unnecessary stress. Be honest: how many meetings or commitments are already on your calendar that you must attend?

After conducting this reality check, you may find that instead of eight hours of work, you have only four hours of focused, uninterrupted time.

Next, establish a clear end-of-day boundary to prevent overworking. Ask yourself: when do I want to wrap up my day? Setting this boundary helps maintain work-life balance.

Break Your Work into Manageable Time Units

Regardless of how large or small a task is, it's always beneficial to divide your time into manageable, predefined slots. The key is finding a unit of time or *timebox* that works for you—whether that's 25 minutes, 45 minutes, or 1–2 hours. This helps you stay focused and in flow while maintaining the flexibility to pause and check emails or jump to other tasks when necessary. This will be your standard **timebox**.

Define a timebox that fits your natural work rhythm. For example, the Pomodoro Technique suggests 25-minute intervals separated by 5 minute breaks, which can be especially effective if you need help maintaining focus or have ADD or ADHD.

I use 45-minute blocks, as most of my meetings are 45 minutes, so my brain gets used to staying focused for 45 or double 90 minutes for complex tasks. Then I always have 15 minutes left (sometimes more, sometimes less) as a transition to rest, check emails and get ready for the next task.

The goal is to work on one task at a time without unnecessary interruption. By predefining your time slots, you create a structure that helps you manage deep work and flexibility.

To track your time, you can use timers, such as the Pomodoro timer or in-app tools like Sunsama, to stay on track. These intervals will help you build momentum, reduce procrastination, and celebrate your progress in a manageable and effective way.

Group Tasks

Break each activity into related task groups and assign each group its own dedicated time and space. For example, if you're planning a presentation, you might spend the morning at your desk gathering information and organizing ideas, the afternoon in a quiet café drafting the slides, and the evening at home rehearsing your delivery. Similarly, group routine tasks—like responding to customer inquiries, scheduling meetings, or processing paperwork—and complete them in one focused session to streamline your day and reduce unnecessary interruptions. This method helps maintain productivity and creates a smoother workflow.

If you need more structure and work from home, try to set up a dedicated office to separate work from personal so you can do all your work stuff there. Once you shut down, you are out of the office. If you have creative tasks, you may leave your office to ramp up creativity.

If you are not very structured, you may need different spaces to work. Choose 2 or 3 spaces in advance that can help you boost your productivity.

Challenge Your Planning

After timeboxing your day, review your plan. Ask yourself: Can I eliminate or delegate any tasks? Can I reduce the time spent on them? Can I postpone some until tomorrow? Keep your schedule realistic. Overcommitting leads to frustration and a sense of underachievement, so strike a balance between ambition and reality.

Follow Your Calendar: Prioritize and Stick to Your Plan

The true power of timeboxing lies in sticking to your plan. Avoid the temptation to shuffle tasks mid-day. If adjustments are necessary, update your calendar to keep accurate records and evaluate your progress at the end of the day. Add additional blocks for new tasks, and move remaining tasks around to later or the next day, but stay aligned with your original priorities.

Timeboxing works best when you do the most important tasks first. That way, if you need to shift things around during the day, you'll have already completed what matters most. Drawing on the Pareto Principle (the 80/20 rule), I recommend tackling the critical 20% of tasks at the start of your day—those tasks that will yield 80% of your desired results. You will learn more about this in the Focus chapter.

Buffers When Shifting Priorities Disrupt Your Day

*"When my schedule is too rigid, there
is no way for me to follow through."*

Shifting priorities and unexpected interruptions—from urgent emails to last-minute requests or tasks that take too long to complete—can quickly derail your plans. How can you manage your time effectively in the face of these relentless distractions?

The key lies not in eliminating these interruptions—yes, work on reducing them, but eliminating them could be nearly impossible—but in creating a flexible structure that can absorb them without overwhelming your schedule. The goal is first finish the 20% critical tasks, and then be ready to shift less critical and unfinished tasks to the following day.

Consider your schedule as a strand of DNA. Just as certain sections in DNA act as buffers to prevent genetic errors (According to current scientific understanding, approximately 98-99% of DNA does not contain genes, meaning it is considered "non-coding" DNA), not every hour of your need needs to be filled with tasks. You can leave blank spaces to check your mails, make personal calls, dedicate more time to critical tasks if needed, or add new responsibilities.

Here are several strategies to help you manage your time and maintain productivity amid constant new tasks and unforeseen changes.

How to Buffer Times Between Meetings

When your day is packed back-to-back, even a slight delay can escalate into stress. Reserve "blank" or open blocks of time for handling last-minute requests and changes in priorities.

This strategy helps you avoid feeling overwhelmed, creating room for flexibility to adapt when urgent tasks arise. By leaving gaps in your schedule, you equip yourself to pivot without disrupting your entire day.

Incorporate buffer times of at least 10 to 15 minutes between meetings to accommodate unexpected disruptions and new tasks. These short breaks allow you to handle urgent items or last-minute requests without compromising workflow. It also enhances the quality of your next meeting, as you can prepare and focus better after a brief pause.

To create a 15-minute buffer between meetings, you have three simple options:

1. Automatic Buffer Settings: Many calendar tools have settings allowing you to add breaks between meetings automatically. The calendar will prevent back-to-back bookings by activating this feature, ensuring a 15-minute gap. This helps create space to wrap up notes, grab a break, or mentally transition before the next meeting.

2. Scheduling Shorter Meetings: Instead of scheduling full 60-minute meetings, you can set them to end at 45 minutes. This approach maintains a 15-minute buffer and encourages a more efficient, focused meeting format.

3. Blocking your calendar: When you plan your day the night before and see a packed schedule, you can proactively block or timebox (set as "busy") any remaining open spaces to prevent last-minute meetings from creeping in. This strategy allows you to reserve time for focused work, task completion, or necessary breaks, ensuring that meetings don't entirely consume your day.

Timeboxing can be challenging at first, but it's one of the most effective ways to regain control of your schedule. If you need personalized guidance to optimize your day, I offer one-on-one coaching to help professionals implement these strategies in a way that works for their needs.

A Timebox for Everything

Timeboxing isn't just about managing tasks—it's about giving each aspect of your life the time and attention it deserves. By creating distinct timeboxes for different activities, you can ensure a balanced and productive day.

Whether it's carving out Power Time for focused work, setting aside Wellbeing Time to recharge your body and mind, or breaking down tasks into 2-Minute Tasks to keep momentum going, timeboxing allows you to optimize your time while reducing stress. Each classification serves a unique purpose, and together, they form a strategy to help you shine in every area of your life.

Timeboxing is also about allocating your mental effort. By compartmentalizing each task, you give yourself permission to focus fully during the designated time and then let it go once it's over. This helps prevent overthinking and stress, allowing you to move on to the next task with clarity.

Small (2-Minute) Tasks

Should you timebox every single task you need to do? The more tasks you put on your calendar, the more realistic your schedule and expectations of the day are. But for quick tasks—those taking just a couple of minutes—either do them immediately (the "Two-Minute Rule"), like responding to an email with a "yes," or "here is the link to my calendar to have a meeting," or group them into a dedicated time block (like a one-hour window every day for all small items). This approach prevents these tiny tasks from cluttering your day, freeing up mental space and reducing the temptation to procrastinate.

Admin Work Blocks' for Managing New Tasks

To combat the nagging feeling that you have to do (but you don't want to) administrative tasks, such as paying invoices, schedule specific blocks of time for administrative work. The goal is to alleviate the mental burden of continuous interruptions. Setting aside 60 to 90 minutes daily or weekly (depending on the amount of work) can help you batch-process communications and tackle incoming tasks rather than reacting to them throughout the day. You can add your two-minute tasks to this block.

You can do the same with email management, setting a "check email" time to prevent continuously checking emails and avoid distractions and switching costs.

Power Time

Everyone has a period during the day when they perform at their best, especially when addressing complex tasks requiring creativity and problem-solving. For many people, this peak moment occurs in the morning, shortly after waking up, when their mental clarity is sharp. However, this varies from person to person. Some might feel their best in the afternoon or even at night, especially if they're naturally more of a night owl. I recently interviewed Cathy Speed, Senior Clinical Specialist at Google Health for one of my Forbes columns[iii]. As an expert in the field, she stated that most of us tend to be more alert in the mornings, more creative in the late afternoon and early evening, and perform our best during late afternoon workouts.

Understanding when you're most alert allows you to use your willpower effectively. Willpower often peaks at the start of the day, but the key is to experiment and discover when you're naturally most productive. Once identified, reserve that "power time" for your most demanding, complex, or high-impact tasks. Enable yourself to make substantial progress at least once a day and fill your day with motivation.

> *"Recognizing your personal "power time"—the period when you're most alert and focused—can further optimize your productivity and overall health".*

Cathy Speed, Senior Clinical Specialist at Google Health

"Me" Time and Prep Time

Finally, ensure you allocate time for unwinding and personal activities that are essential to your wellbeing. Timeboxing isn't just for work. Schedule breaks, workouts, relaxation, or commute time and personal projects into your calendar. You can also reserve time before and after meetings for preparation and follow-up. Incorporating activities you enjoy boosts motivation, reduces stress, and helps maintain a healthy balance.

Focus on intentionally filling each hour with tasks that align with your goals and personal wellbeing. Prioritize activities, even small ones, that are both relevant and rewarding. Adding them to your calendar—even if they're not strictly work-related—can enhance your focus and motivation, providing a boost from satisfying, balanced progress. Examples of these rewarding tasks could be working on an important personal project, reading a book, playing an instrument, or studying. These activities help stimulate beneficial hormones, like dopamine and endorphins, which support productivity, reduce stress, and promote sustained momentum to tackle the rest of your day.

Wellbeing Time

You may be surprised that I recommend timeboxing **Wellbeing Time**—especially exercise. I have had this conversation with many coachees, and most of them say they want to keep life and work separate, so they've never thought about scheduling time for a workout. But I genuinely feel that keeping them on your calendar timeboxed helps to keep them visible without affecting your work priorities. You have the reminder to do it and take it seriously.

While you may already appreciate that exercise enhances productivity and overall wellbeing, finding time for a full workout can seem daunting. The good news is that short, 5- to 10-minute bursts of activity, or "exercise snacks," throughout your day can deliver substantial physical and mental benefits—without disrupting your busy schedule.

Traditional exercise is often seen as an hour-long gym session or an early morning routine, but research shows that even 10–15 minutes of distributed activity can combat fatigue, increase energy, and enhance focus. Whether it's a brisk walk, some stretching, or a few bodyweight exercises, these mini-sessions can help activate muscles, improve metabolism, and boost mental clarity.

Relying solely on an evening gym session may not be enough to counteract the negative impacts of prolonged sitting. Cathy Speed emphasized, "There are two key elements to consider: keeping your body active throughout the day and performing planned bursts of more focused exercise. Neither one replaces the other."

Prolonged inactivity contributes to obesity, cardiometabolic diseases, musculoskeletal problems, and it can also diminish concentration and motivation. Even a few minutes of activity—like squats or jumping jacks—can make a noticeable difference. Innovative features, such as Fitbit's Cardio Load, now allow users to monitor how hard their heart works during these brief sessions, ensuring a balanced approach between exercise duration and intensity.

Since the onset of the pandemic, I've become a strong advocate for 10-minute exercise sessions. I started by exploring short, targeted workouts online, such as Pamela Reif's—focusing on core strength and overall conditioning— and gradually integrated them with my regular tennis and swimming routines. Instead of setting aside a full hour for exercise—which I often can't do daily—I opt for quick 10-minute bursts, or "exercise snacks."

Recently, I began monitoring my heart rate more closely, which led me to incorporate higher-intensity bursts into my 10-minute workouts to optimize my cardio load and maintain a high overall fitness level, even during busy times.

When it comes to choosing exercises, convenience and consistency are paramount. Here are some strategies to incorporate movement into your workday:

- **Desk-Friendly Workouts:** Keep light weights at your desk or use a jump rope during breaks.
- **Active Meetings:** If you're in back-to-back online webinars or conference calls, consider using a treadmill or stationary bike.
- **Simple Movement Breaks:** Opt for quick activities like walking around the office, taking the stairs, or doing a set of jumping jacks or squats.
- **Mindful Routines:** Dedicate even 2 minutes—either before bed or upon waking—to breathing exercises. Dr. Amanda Paluch[iv], kinesiologist and assistant professor at the University of Massachusetts Amherst School of Public Health and Health Sciences, notes, "Those who prioritize both fitness and mindfulness will likely see the best results in improving their physical and mental health and overall quality of life."

Integrating regular movement into your workday is a simple yet powerful strategy to enhance mental and physical health. By incorporating brief exercise breaks, leveraging fitness data, and aligning your schedule with your body's natural rhythms, you can unlock significant improvements in performance. Even minimal, consistent efforts can lead to lasting, positive transformations in your productivity and overall health.

Plan the Big Picture

Sometimes, breaking your day into individual tasks can feel overwhelming. Instead, try categorizing your day into four distinct blocks, making it easier to manage your time and focus:

1. **Meeting / Team Time:** Scheduled interactions, collaboration, and communication with others.
2. **Power Time:** Focused, uninterrupted periods for complex, engaging tasks requiring concentration and problem-solving.
3. **2-Minute Tasks / Admin tasks:** Quick, simple tasks like emails, phone calls, or administrative duties that can be completed quickly.
4. **Me / Wellbeing Time**: Time for self-care activities like exercise, breaks, meals, or moments of relaxation to recharge.

By organizing your day into these four categories, you understand what needs to be done and when. The key is to stay within these "buckets," which helps prevent distractions and promotes a balanced, focused approach to the day.

Emotional Shifts to Embrace Timeboxing with Compassion

Timeboxing isn't just about managing your schedule—it's about creating emotional clarity. The fundamental emotional shift with timeboxing is learning to set realistic expectations for what you can truly accomplish in a day. Rather than feeling overwhelmed by an endless to-do list, timeboxing teaches you to break tasks into manageable chunks, decide which ones are achievable today, and allocate the mental energy needed for each.

By compartmentalizing each task, you give yourself permission to focus entirely during the designated time and then let it go once the block is over. This reduces the emotional weight of unfinished tasks hanging over you and stops the cycle of overthinking that often leads to stress and burnout. You move on to the next task with clarity, knowing you gave your best effort in the previous one.

To illustrate, it's like when I play tennis. I tell myself, "I just need to get the ball over the net," and once I make the shot, I focus on positioning myself for the next play. If I keep watching the ball to see whether it stays in the court or if my opponent gets it, I miss the opportunity to prepare for what's next. The same goes for timeboxing: once you complete a task, move on with purpose, trusting that you've done your best.

✦ PRO TIP: Set expectations for what you *need* to do, but for what you *can* do, considering your current resources, mental energy, and time. Timeboxing lets you approach your day with compassion, understanding that you are human, and there will always be more to do. Instead of trying to conquer the entire list, timeboxing helps you focus on one thing at a time, with full attention, then allow yourself to move on. It's not about perfection—it's about intentionality and balance.

Putting a task on your calendar moves it from your head to action. This simple step helps take away the mental clutter.

What's Next

Timeboxing is a simple concept, but it can be challenging to execute. You might skip your schedule, work overtime, or spend too much time on a task. This isn't a sign of failure—it's simply part of the adaptation process. To make timeboxing a lasting habit, follow the "3Fs" of time management. Every time you approach a task, pass through these three stages:

1. **Focus**: Start by choosing one task and commit to it. Eliminate distractions, and let go of concerns about what's coming next.
2. **Flow**: Engage deeply with the task, aiming for a state of concentration where time seems to slip away. Enjoy the process and the progress you're making.
3. **Finish**: Complete the task before moving on to the next one. Aim for "good enough" rather than perfection, and celebrate your progress.

As you delve into each of these three stages in the coming chapters, remember to treat yourself with self-compassion. You'll learn how to **timebox on your calendar but also compartmentalize in your mind**—letting go of emotions when switching between tasks. Building new habits takes time, and setbacks are a natural part of the process. By staying patient, kind, and understanding toward yourself, you'll foster a healthier mindset, making it easier to integrate timeboxing into your daily life.

Takeaways

- **Timebox**: A method for managing tasks by allocating fixed blocks of time to work on specific activities, ensuring focus and productivity without overwhelming yourself.
- **Buffer Time**: Short breaks or flexibility built into your schedule between power time blocks to reset, reflect, or adjust for delays or unexpected interruptions.
- **2-Minute Tasks**: Small, quick tasks grouped in a dedicated time block instead of scattered throughout your day.
- **Power Time**: The focused, uninterrupted period when you fully concentrate on a task. It should be used for high-priority or complex tasks when you need to be the most productive.
- **Prep Time Blocks**: Adding extra time around meetings for preparation and post-meeting tasks.
- **Me / Wellbeing Time**: Time for self-care activities like exercise, breaks, meals, or moments of relaxation to recharge.

Practical Tips to Cultivate Compassionate Timeboxing TODAY

- **Timebox with compassion:** plan today what you will work on tomorrow by scheduling your most urgent and important tasks into your calendar, including one task you love or "me" time.
- **Curious Flexibility:** Allocate time for breaks and 15' empty buckets for unexpected interruptions, allowing flexibility in your schedule.

Download the worksheet for this chapter at
www.lucypaulise.com/timebox

Chapter 5 | FOCUS
What needs to be done now?

How to concentrate on what truly matters.

> *"I want to be a resource to others,*
> *but I struggle with saying no. When I can't*
> *focus on one thing, it takes hours from my*
> *family and forces me to work late. I wear*
> *too many hats and overextend myself."*

Focus is the antithesis of multitasking. It involves dedicating undivided attention to a single task. In today's distracted world, cultivating focus is essential for productivity and wellbeing. This chapter will explore how to harness focus and overcome the barriers that fragment our time.

The Unfortunate Reality of Time Fragmentation

Time fragmentation occurs when your day splits into countless tiny tasks, preventing the deep focus needed for significant progress. Emails, meetings, and notifications carve the workday into disjointed intervals, leaving you wondering where the time went and why so little got done. The "always on" mentality forces partial attention to everything and, thus, full attention to nothing. A fractured day reduces impact and wellbeing.

When you see a big to-do list, you may feel like you must do it all now. So, instead of deciding what to do first, you tend to do several things simultaneously to "gain time," so you multitask.

Research shows that it takes around 20 minutes[v] to regain focus on the original task when distracted. Constantly switching between tasks wastes time, leads to more mistakes, and reduces memory retention. Some clients say they sometimes feel "sick" and "overwhelmed" doing tasks they love.

Whether you're an entrepreneur, remote worker, or corporate professional, the ability to concentrate on a critical task at a time and have longer blocks of time for similar things can transform your productivity and career. By embracing focus, you can regain control, combat time fragmentation, and prioritize the tasks that truly matter.

The Power of Focus

Deep concentration is the antidote to fragmentation. Focus involves[vi] directing your undivided attention and mental resources to a single task or goal. When you fully commit to a task, you often enter a flow state—something we will explore in the next chapter. However, flow is unattainable without focus. Beyond enhancing productivity, focus boosts your sense of accomplishment, elevates your mood, and contributes to overall wellbeing. Ultimately, it leads to a more satisfying and fulfilling work experience. The power of focus lies in harnessing your mental energy and attention on a single task, eliminating distractions and improving productivity.

When you focus, you create a clear path to achieve your goals by:

1. **Enhancing Productivity:** Focused work leads to faster completion of tasks because your energy is concentrated on one thing at a time.
2. **Deepening Concentration:** When you are entirely focused, you enter a state of deep work that fosters creativity, problem-solving, and higher-quality output.
3. **Reducing Stress:** By focusing on what's in front of you, you avoid feeling overwhelmed by the entire workload, which can reduce anxiety and increase confidence.
4. **Improving Decision-Making:** Clear focus helps you make better decisions, as you are not distracted by irrelevant information or competing tasks.
5. **Building Momentum:** Focusing on small, manageable tasks builds momentum, like a positive snowball effect, leading to more extraordinary accomplishments over time.

The power of focus isn't just about staying on task—it's about channeling your energy toward meaningful progress.

Common Reasons People Struggle to Focus

Identifying which triggers affect you most is the first step toward improving your ability to focus. Some common triggers for a lack of focus include:

- The belief that you are more effective when multitasking
- Frequent notifications and distractions
- Disorganized work environments
- Feeling overwhelmed or anxious
- ADHD or other attention-related challenges
- Lack of connection to long-term goals

Question for you
What are your primary triggers for losing focus?
Can you prioritize them so that you have your primary triggers at the top?

Common Challenges From Lack of Focus: Multitasking and Analysis Paralysis

When faced with overwhelm, people either freeze or multitask. Freezing paralyzes progress, while multitasking dilutes effectiveness. Both behaviors stem from a fear of making the wrong decision or a lack of confidence in what is more important.

You are figuring out where to start, thinking about its impact. All the tasks may seem equally important to you, so instead of trusting your decision-making process, you prefer someone else to decide what to work on. What if your perspective needs to be corrected? What if you make a mistake? These are all potentially terrifying outcomes.

But also, you fear asking for help, as you fear bothering other people. For example, you may not reach out to someone with a question, so try to do it yourself. If you have trouble saying no, you change the task based on the latest request and multitask. The results are feelings of anxiety and frustration, not being able to move forward. You are frozen in fear and overthinking. Overthinking makes you spend much longer on the task than you expected. Or you get so frustrated and defeated that you get disengaged at work and do all your tasks haphazardly or half-heartedly.

Challenge #1: Multitasking

Multitasking is often celebrated as a sign of efficiency, but in reality, it fragments your attention and erodes the quality of your work. Instead of immersing yourself deeply in one task, you juggle multiple activities without truly excelling. This constant switching slows you down and increases stress and mental fatigue.

One key benefit of timeboxing is that it encourages you to monotask—complete one assignment at a time, as you should never have two boxes simultaneously. Even if you can't fully finish something due to external constraints, the aim is to keep the number of tasks in progress to a minimum.

Your Coping Mechanism: In moments of stress or overwhelm, you overcompensate by multitasking without planning based on other people's agendas.

Challenge #2: Freeze (Not Starting at All)

At the opposite end of the spectrum from multitasking lies "freeze"—the state of doing nothing at all because starting seems too daunting. While multitasking scatters your efforts, freeze immobilizes you, preventing any meaningful progress. It can happen when tasks feel overwhelming, unclear, or too large to tackle. You don't know what to focus on, so you start worrying and feeling guilty.

Just as timeboxing helps limit the chaos of multitasking, it can also help you by telling you exactly what to work on and, when encouraging you to take that vital first step, gradually thawing the paralysis so you can begin—and eventually complete—your work.

Your Coping Mechanism: In moments of stress or overwhelm, you may "freeze" or surrender, feeling paralyzed and unable to act.

Question for you

How would you rate your focus, from 1 (not focused at all) to 10 (amazingly focused)?

Behavioral Shifts to Maximize Focus

Now that you understand what might be causing time fragmentation and reducing your ability to concentrate on one thing at a time, it's time to take action. The following suggestions aren't rigid, step-by-step instructions. Instead, think of them as tools you can pick and choose from depending on your situation. What helps when you're bored may differ from what helps when you're overwhelmed. The key is to remain self-aware, experimenting with different techniques to find what works best for you.

The 4Ds: Save 75% of Your Time by Doing Less

The million-dollar question is how to prioritize tasks based on urgency and importance. You can use a tool like the Eisenhower Matrix to categorize tasks into four groups: urgent and important, important but not urgent, urgent but not important, and neither urgent nor important. To simplify this process, I use a method called the 4Ds.

- **Do Now**: Focus on urgent and important tasks that require immediate attention or completion.
- **Do Later**: Schedule important but not urgent tasks for later.
- **Delegate**: Pass on urgent but less important tasks to others who can handle them.
- **Delete**: Eliminate tasks that aren't worth your time at all.

By applying the 4Ds, you'll stop trying to power through 100% of your tasks and start focusing on the 25% that truly matter. Do you feel lighter already? Imagine the relief of realizing you only need to tackle a quarter of the things you thought you *had* to do today.

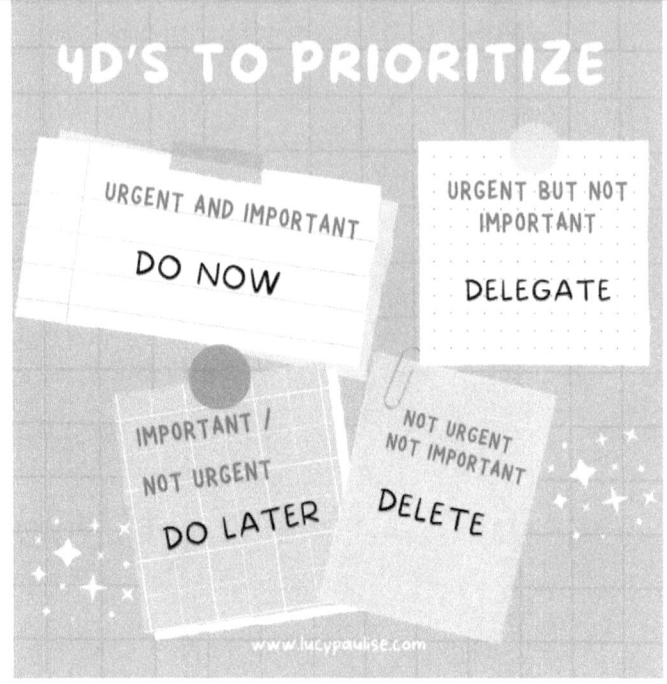

Eisenhower matrix

Visualizing Your Priorities

Picture your day as a jar waiting to be filled with rocks—tasks, projects, and meetings. But how can you fit in the most without overflowing?

Stephen R. Covey, in *The 7 Habits of Highly Effective People*[vii], used the jar metaphor to illustrate the importance of prioritization in time management, emphasizing the need to focus on what matters most.

Instead of randomly adding tasks of all sizes, start with the biggest, most important "rocks." Once these are in place, add smaller tasks ("pebbles" and "sand") to fill the gaps. This method ensures that you focus on what matters most rather than simply doing more.

But how do you prioritize without feeling overwhelmed? Here is where the combination of the rocks and pebbles metaphor, the Eisenhower Matrix, and the 4D system come together to help you manage your time with intention and compassion.

Do Now: Prioritize Urgent and Important Tasks

Start by identifying the big rocks in your backlog—the urgent and important tasks to achieving your North Star or long-term purpose. These high-impact tasks should take up most of your focus because they drive meaningful progress in your work and life.

The Eisenhower Matrix can help you categorize tasks, distinguishing between what is urgent and important and what feels pressing but doesn't contribute to your bigger goals. The key is to avoid the common mistake of thinking everything is a "Do Now." That's when multitasking takes over, or worse, you freeze and accomplish nothing.

I know it's overwhelming, but here's the challenge: choose only one or two tasks that absolutely require immediate action. That's it. Taking on too many "Do Now" tasks at once will only lead to burnout and inefficiency. Focus on these priority tasks first, and you'll gain momentum without feeling paralyzed by the weight of your to-do list.

By clearly identifying your available time after doing these Do Now tasks, you can prioritize other tasks in your backlog, 3D (do later, delegate, or delete) and set yourself up for success without overloading your day.

Do Later: Important But Not Urgent

Once you've prioritized your **Do Now** tasks, it's time to consider the smaller, less urgent tasks—the pebbles and sand that still contribute to your productivity but don't require immediate attention. These tasks are necessary, but don't carry the same weight as the big rocks and can be scheduled for later without impacting your immediate priorities.

Instead of letting these tasks clutter your focus, timebox them for a specific time in your day or week so they don't get lost or pile up. By intentionally scheduling them, you ensure they get done without interfering with your high-impact work.

Examples of **Do Later** tasks include:

✓ **Strategic planning** (e.g., updating your LinkedIn profile, brainstorming ideas for a project)

✓ **Long-term projects** (e.g., developing a new product, preparing for an important meeting next week)

✓ **Routine administrative work** (e.g., organizing files, responding to non-urgent emails)

By **timeboxing these tasks**, you create **dedicated space for them without the mental burden** of keeping them top-of-mind. This allows you to stay present with your current priorities while knowing you have a plan to tackle everything else at the right time.

Delegate: Not Important but Urgent

If a task is urgent but not critical to your direct involvement, consider reassigning it, collaborating with a colleague with the capacity or expertise or empowering others in your team. These tasks may be important—but not necessarily *for you* to complete.

Sharing responsibilities helps reduce your workload while also encouraging collaboration and professional growth within the team. You must make conscious choices about what to prioritize to keep your jar from overflowing. Instead of trying to fit everything in, focus on filling your jar with rocks that align with your goals.

Delete: Not Important and not Urgent

If a task isn't worth your time, **let it go.** When you first added it to your list, it might have seemed important or interesting, but priorities shift. Holding onto low-value tasks only clutters your backlog and drains your mental energy.

We often keep quick and easy tasks because completing them gives us a sense of progress—like listening to a trendy podcast, signing up for yet another online course, or researching something that isn't necessary. But **does it align with your North Star?** If the answer is no, it's time to **drop it.**

The sooner you **eliminate unnecessary tasks**, the cleaner and more effective your backlog becomes. This frees up your time and focus on what truly matters, ensuring that every task on your list contributes to your goals rather than just keeping you busy.

To avoid overflowing your jar, choose carefully which big rocks (your most important and urgent tasks) to fit in first. Then, consider what is pebbles and sand (those smaller tasks you can fill in with the remaining time, not important and not urgent), and which "rocks" you can give to your neighbor, throw away, or put in the jar tomorrow. When you have more space in the jar, you can maintain a to-do list or backlog with rocks to choose from tomorrow.

How to Focus on What Matters Most: Identify Your "Do Now" Tasks

As discussed earlier with the Eisenhower Matrix, not all tasks are equal. To significantly impact your goals, start by identifying and scheduling time for your "Do Now" tasks. These are your most important and high-impact tasks—often urgent, complex, and requiring your full attention. Focusing on these "big rocks" will yield significant results and help you make real progress.

Focusing on these critical tasks offers several advantages:

- **Strategic Impact**: "Do Now" tasks are the ones that align with your long-term goals and can push your career or projects forward in meaningful ways.
- **Time Efficiency**: By first addressing the most critical tasks, you prevent smaller, less significant items from taking up your time and avoid time fragmentation.
- **Motivation and Satisfaction**: Completing a major task brings a tangible sense of accomplishment, which can reduce feelings of overwhelm and build momentum for the rest of your day.

Apply the Pareto Principle

An Italian economist, Vilfredo Pareto, discovered what's now known as the **Pareto Principle**, or the **80/20 Rule**, which states that 80% of results come from 20% of efforts. Initially observed in wealth distribution, this rule applies to many areas of life, including time management. In terms of your daily tasks, it suggests that 20% of what you do will yield 80% of your results.

By applying this principle, you can prioritize your most vital tasks and filter out the less important ones. Use the Pareto Rule to identify what matters, and don't hesitate to say no to tasks or requests that don't align with your core objectives. The goal is to focus on what's truly worth your time.

Identifying the Vital Few

To apply the 80/20 rule effectively, start by analyzing your daily tasks and responsibilities. If you work 8 to 10 hours a day, consider how much time is spent in meetings, eating lunch, exercising, handling administrative tasks, or engaging in brief activities. Among all these tasks, identify the 20-25% that impact your success most. These are your "big rocks" or "vital few"—the crucial activities that drive you closer to your goals. In terms of the Eisenhower Matrix, these are your **"Do Now" tasks**, the top 20-25% of priorities that demand your immediate focus and attention.

Think about it this way: You can't excel at everything. Consider your workload as if it were a set of subjects in school. What are the 20% of subjects in which you can achieve an A+ that will generate 80% of your results because they will be part of your career in the long term? And what are the other 80% of subjects where a C+ is acceptable? By focusing on the "vital few," you can maximize your results while allowing yourself to let go of perfection in less impactful areas.

✦ PRO TIP: Choose a 2-hour task that would make you feel satisfied to complete by the end of the day. For example, specific clients could drive most of your revenue, high-impact projects that shape your career, like writing a code to fix a problem or key relationships that open doors. Focusing on these high-priority tasks will significantly increase your effectiveness and yield the greatest results.

While you dedicate 2 hours of focused time to your highest-priority tasks, the remaining hours of your day should still be used wisely. This is where the remaining 80% of tasks come into play—these are your "less critical" tasks that, while necessary, don't need the same level of effort or intense focus.

Delegate the Trivial Many

Next, identify the less critical tasks—what's known as the "trivial many"—that take up most of your time and are not as impactful. The remaining 80% of your tasks often fall into ths category. These tasks can be broken down using the 3 Ds—**Do Later**, **Delegate**, or **Delete**—to help streamline your day and focus only on what truly moves the needle. These are the tasks that, while necessary, are less critical and don't need to be completed immediately or by you personally. Streamline your workflows by eliminating or reducing these tasks, when someone else can execute them. It could be not always answering your Slack when other coworkers can collaborate or saying NO to some projects. You aim to do more of what you are great at and set aside uninterrupted time to ensure you complete your "Do Now" tasks.

Protect Your Power Time

Consider blocking at least two uninterrupted hours dedicated to these vital tasks: your "power time."

Protect this time from distractions—a phone call, meeting, or email—and treat it as a non-negotiable appointment. Creating dedicated time slots for your most essential tasks will significantly improve your concentration and productivity.

Establishing a consistent routine helps train your body and mind to expect and support deep focus simultaneously each day or week. Once you identify your "power time," make it a permanent fixture in your calendar—daily or weekly—to ensure you're consistently dedicating time to your most critical work.

This focus period doesn't need to be long, but consistency is key. The more regularly you structure your day around your power hours, the easier it becomes to dive into complex tasks confidently. Not only does this increase your ability to concentrate, but it also builds momentum, allowing you to accomplish more in less time.

Willpower is the mental energy that powers your focus and decision-making. It's at its peak when you're well-rested and mentally refreshed, ready to tackle high-priority projects that demand your full attention. By identifying and protecting your "power time," you harness your most valuable resource—your focus—and maximize your productivity.

Once this routine becomes ingrained, you'll find it easier to concentrate over time.

Time Chunking: Break Big Tasks into Manageable Pieces

As mentioned in the previous chapter, large projects can feel overwhelming and lead to procrastination. You may also be frustrated by how long they take to complete, only celebrating once everything is finished. By dividing big projects into smaller, more achievable milestones, you transform them from intimidating to manageable. This approach lets you track daily progress, appreciate each step forward, and maintain steady momentum.

Try working in shorter intervals that suit your style and attention span. For example, use the 25-minute Pomodoro technique (25 minutes of work and 5 minutes of rest for each cycle), one-hour blocks, or another comfortable time segment. These smaller, more focused chunks of work are more manageable to start and finish, boosting your motivation and concentration.

I usually break my day into 45-minute chunks. When tackling complex or creative tasks like writing, I often block two 45-minute chunks back-to-back to leverage sustained focus and extend my productive period, and leave 15 minutes free to pause, relax, etc. or workout.

Keep the Task Visible

When multitasking, it's easy to lose track of what you're doing. That's why it's important to keep the task you're working on visible to remind you where you are. Timeboxing keeps tasks visible on your calendar. Post-its, whiteboards, focus modes, or apps like Sunsama can keep your current task front and center, helping you resist the urge to switch tasks prematurely. Try keeping less tabs open or working on one tab at a time.

One powerful way to maintain visibility and focus on your tasks is by using a Kanban board. This simple yet highly effective tool helps you manage work in progress and visually track tasks as you move through them. It's particularly useful when juggling multiple tasks simultaneously, as it highlights your workload and shows if you're attempting to take on too much.

A Kanban board is a visual management tool originally developed in Japan for workflow and task management. It's typically divided into several columns representing stages of a task's progress. These stages usually include "To Do," "In Progress," and "Done," but can be customized to fit your workflow. Tasks are represented by cards or sticky notes that move across the board from left to right as they progress through the workflow.

The main idea behind a Kanban board is to limit the number of tasks in progress at any given time, encouraging focus, reducing the risk of multitasking overload, and helping ensure you finish tasks before starting new ones. It provides a clear visual representation of your current workload, so you can immediately see what's been completed, what's in progress, and what still needs attention.

A personal Kanban board can take many forms, depending on your preferences and needs. It could be a simple app or an Excel spreadsheet with three columns: "To Do," "In Progress," and "Done." You update this board daily to keep track of your tasks and progress. Alternatively, it could be as basic as a bin or folder labeled "Open Items," either physically on your desk or digitally as a folder on your desktop. This serves as a catch-all for tasks that need completion, providing a clear overview of what still requires attention.

Some tasks, like drafting emails or writing proposals, may require you to step away and revisit them after reflection before finalizing them. Each draft can be represented by a separate card in your "In Progress" column or stored in your "In Progress" folder. I sometimes add **DO NOW** at the beginning of the document name to easily remember where I was working.

Having a dedicated space for work in progress helps you stay focused on one task at a time, preventing you from jumping between multiple projects. It also serves as a helpful reminder of what is still pending, ensuring nothing slips through the cracks.

The 5-Minute Rule: Overcoming Resistance and Building Momentum

One of the biggest challenges when the temptation is to multitask is getting started on one thing at a time. Whether the task feels too dull, daunting, or overwhelming, the hardest part is often just making the first move. That's where the 5-Minute Rule comes in—a simple yet powerful strategy for overcoming the inertia that prevents you from diving into your work.

The 5-Minute Rule is based on a simple commitment: **if a task feels too much to handle, commit just five minutes to it.** Setting aside the pressure to finish the task and simply focusing on starting reduces the resistance that can stop you. Often, the hardest part is simply getting the ball rolling. Once you begin, you'll usually find that the task is not as daunting as it seemed and that you can continue easily.

Even if you stop after just five minutes, you've made progress. This small effort reduces the mental barrier for the next time you approach that task, making it easier to begin again. You're also building momentum by engaging with the task, even briefly. The brain responds to this momentum, and what seemed like a daunting project can often feel much more manageable.

Additionally, committing to only five minutes can reduce the feeling of being overwhelmed, which often paralyzes people from starting. Instead of focusing on the enormity of the task, you break it down into a small, achievable chunk of time. Once you've completed those five minutes, you may realize that the task is not as unmanageable as it first appeared, and you're in a better position to continue and get into the flow state of this book's next chapter.

This rule is beneficial when you're trying to break through the resistance that many of us face at the beginning of a task. Resistance is a natural part of the work process, but it doesn't have to keep you from entering flow later on. By taking that first small step, the 5-Minute Rule lets you bypass the initial friction and gain the momentum needed to dive deeper into your work.

Try it with your kids if you want to urge them to do homework, read a book or study a second language.

How to Use the 5-Minute Rule to Enter Flow:
1. **Set a Timer**: Commit to spending just five minutes on the task. The short time frame makes it feel less intimidating.
2. **Start Small**: Focus on starting, not finishing. Allow yourself to complete just a portion of the task without worrying about the end result.

3. **Observe the Momentum**: After five minutes, pause and decide whether to continue. Most of the time, starting will naturally lead you into a deeper focus and eventually flow.

"Just One Thing": A Simple Way to Boost Focus and Motivation

In a recent conversation with one of my coachees, we explored ways to increase his motivation. We discovered that every day, he was only working on tasks others needed from him, leaving no room for his own goals or personal needs.

To address this, I suggested he focus on one thing per day—a small, achievable task he could complete in 15 or 30 minutes. This change was eye-opening for him. By narrowing his focus, he felt less overwhelmed and more motivated. This approach works exceptionally well for people-pleasers or parents who prioritize others' needs over their own.

If this sounds like you, there's no harm in deciding to focus on just one thing you enjoy each day. While it is nothing wrong to put others' needs first, it can be draining and demotivating over time. Doing things that matter to you can boost your energy dramatically.

Whether it's getting some exercise, reading a book chapter, or finally tackling something you've been procrastinating on, permit yourself to prioritize that task for a short, dedicated period.

✦ PRO TIP: We agreed that he would write his "one thing" on a Post-it each morning to make the process more visual and celebrate progress. After completing it, he'd toss the post-it into a cup. He also shared pictures of his progress with me over time, reinforcing his commitment.

This simple practice helps break the cycle of overwhelm, allowing you to regain control over your day, feel accomplished, and stay focused on what matters to you.

"I felt relieved and more motivated when I realized I only needed to focus on one thing daily. I didn't need to think about tasks 24/7—just 30 minutes was enough."

Do The Hardest Thing First

In her book *The CBT Workbook for Perfectionism*[viii], Sharon Martin recommends starting with the most challenging thing when you feel stuck. She explains that "most people are inclined to do the easiest thing on their to-do list," which is why your most important but complex tasks are often undone. To overcome this freeze mode, tackle the most challenging thing, especially if your power time is in the morning. Make sure to prioritize what matters most.

As I mentioned earlier in the book, having breakfast and getting ready often took an hour of my precious time while my daughter was still sleeping. This was a time I could have used to pour my heart into writing first thing in the morning when my ideas were fresh. Even though I'm an unconditional breakfast eater, I found it incredibly productive to use my first hour awake to write without interruptions.

The Stress-Reducing Power of Checking Email Less Frequently

Email has become a cornerstone of professional communication, yet it's also a significant source of poor time management and stress. According to the McKinsey Global Institute, the average professional spends about 28%[ix] of their workday reading and responding to emails, which amounts to more than 11 hours per week.

According to a survey, about one-third of US workers responded within 15 minutes of receiving a work email, and three-fourths replied within an hour. Constant email notifications can be overwhelming, leading to increased stress and reduced productivity due to time fragmentation.

However, research offers a compelling case for why checking email less frequently can significantly reduce stress and improve wellbeing.

The Cognitive Overload of Continuous Checking

Driven by the fear of missing important messages or staying constantly updated, you may check emails continually. This behavior is often exacerbated by push notifications, which create steady interruptions throughout the day. A recent study[x] showed that their participants spent an average of almost one and a half hours per day on email and checked their email an average of 77 times daily.

Each time you switch tasks to check your inbox, your brain requires time to refocus on the original task. This constant task-switching reduces efficiency, leading to cognitive overload and difficulty maintaining deep focus. The result? You might feel busy all day but struggle to complete meaningful tasks.

Kushlev and Dunn[xi], researchers at the University of British Columbia, conducted a study to explore the relationship between email management practices and stress levels. They recruited participants from various professional backgrounds and divided them into two groups. One group was instructed to check their email frequently throughout the day, while the other was asked to limit their email checks to three times daily. The study spanned two weeks, with participants switching email habits midway.

The study found that participants who checked their email less frequently reported significantly lower stress levels than those who continuously checked their email. This stress reduction was attributed to the decreased pressure to be constantly available and responsive. Limiting email checks led to an overall improvement in participants' wellbeing. Those who checked their email less frequently experienced fewer distractions and were better able to focus on their tasks, leading to a sense of accomplishment and satisfaction.

Practical Tips For A More Productive Email Management System

While you may think it's impossible to reduce the volume of emails you receive, some training and tips on email management can help you reduce the stress and distractions. Research by Klaus Moser[xii] confirmed that a training program in effective email management can reduce information overload and its negative consequences.

Checking email is part of our daily routine. Taking control of it to make it less stressful and disruptive of other activities can help you achieve the state of flow, be more productive and lead to a more balanced and fulfilling professional life.

Disable Notifications

First, turn off email notifications on all your devices to reduce the temptation to constantly check your inbox. This simple step can help you stay focused and reduce anxiety.

Batch Email Time

Schedule specific times during the day to check and respond to emails, but from now on, only use your "check email" times[xiii]. You could do this once in the morning, at midday, and then again in the late afternoon. In his book "The 4-Hour Workweek," Tim Ferriss[xiv] suggests checking emails twice a day at set times, while researchers at the University of British Columbia recommend checking them three times a day.

By batching your email activity rather than letting your inbox dictate your schedule, you can reduce the cognitive load associated with frequent task-switching. This approach allows you to focus solely on your emails during these periods, process messages efficiently, and then return to your tasks with a clear mind.

If you need to respond more often, you can also check your emails after a specific trigger, such as after a meeting. Personally, like I mentioned, I schedule my meetings for 45 minutes instead of 60 minutes to always have a buffer between meetings to check emails or reset.

Batch emails by natural interruptions

Despite all the research and data showing the benefits of batching email checking, transitioning from checking emails 77 times a day to just three can seem unrealistic for many, especially if there's a fear of missing out on important communications.

A recent study published by Gloria Mark[xv] shows that a more flexible and effective strategy is to align your email checking with the natural rhythm of your workday. Instead of adhering to strict, predetermined intervals, you can check your emails after completing specific tasks. This approach minimizes the disruption to your focus and flow, as you're not breaking your concentration mid-task but rather using the completion of one task as a natural cue to address your inbox.

For example, if you've just finished drafting a report or completing a time-boxed task, checking and responding to emails can feel like a natural and productive pause before moving on to your next task. This method is particularly beneficial for those who work on projects that require deep concentration. You create a seamless transition between activities by checking emails during these natural breaks without compromising your focus.

This strategy also helps alleviate the feeling that you might miss something important in your inbox. By checking emails regularly but not excessively, you can stay on top of your communications without allowing them to dominate your day. This way, you better balance your task-oriented work and email management, leading to higher productivity and lower stress levels.

Incorporating this approach into your daily routine can significantly improve your time and energy management. By letting your tasks dictate when you check your inbox—rather than the other way around—you empower yourself to maintain control over your workday, boosting your efficiency and wellbeing.

✦ PRO TIP: Batch your emails by natural interruptions. Combining this with the idea of buffers and reducing meeting times, turn all your meetings and events into 45-minute blocks (instead of 1-hour slots). This gives you a 15-minute buffer to regroup—whether it's for a quick break, to adjust if a meeting runs late, to jot down any important thoughts that might distract you later, or to check emails and notifications.

Learn more about email management in the chapter *BONUS TIPS.*

Yes, Notifications are Your #1 Distraction

Out of all the ways mentioned above to reduce distractions, the most accessible and challenging at the same time is reducing notifications. It's easy to get sucked into the endless stream of notifications and messages, causing a significant impact on productivity. Most of the time, I hear that the excuse to leave notifications on is because it is part of your work, and you always have to stay on.

That is why I want to tackle this issue specifically and share some strategies to reduce distractions and improve productivity.

One of the main problems I have seen with Slack, emails, and other messages is that when you have questions posted that you can answer, you almost feel obligated to answer them immediately. This sounds like a very collaborative approach, though on the other hand, being always available hinders your own productivity[xvi], your ability to focus, and your presence in life outside work. What if you reframe your priorities and obligations? Staying always on doesn't necessarily mean replying within 3 seconds (unless stated explicitly by your employer). You can also stay on by focusing 30 minutes on something and then checking your emails. Prioritize what types of messages you should respond to, which ones are not necessarily your responsibility, and set times to be intentionally available to help others. Just like I shared, you can use natural interruptions to check emails or the same to check any notifications.

✦ PRO TIP: It's essential to establish specific times when you'll be available based on the priorities set before and when you won't. Communicate these boundaries with your team to let them know when they can expect your response. Timebox your availability on your calendar to make it more explicit for you and others. Additionally, you can set your status to let people know when you're unavailable or busy with work. Define what is required from each of you as a team to ensure the job is done, but you also have focus time.

Take the time to customize the setting based on, realistically, when and how often you receive notifications. You can adjust settings to mute channels or conversations that aren't essential to your work and set specific notification preferences for each channel. This way, you'll only receive notifications for important messages, reducing distractions and increasing productivity.

✦ PRO TIP: "Do Not Disturb" mode lets you turn off notifications entirely during specific times. You can set it up to turn on automatically during work hours on your computer, phone or any particular app, which means you won't receive any notifications. It will allow you to focus on your work and avoid multitasking for a specific period. For instance, I like using the "do not disturb all day" option and only reviewing notifications based on my timeboxed calendar and natural breaks. Once I finish a task, I check for messages. That is why I always recommend timeboxing in small chunks, at most 1 or 2 hours long. Establishing time to focus on strategic work increases that feeling of flow, creativity, and satisfaction, which can boost your workday and improve your time management skills.

Use integrations and AI

I've discussed this with many coachees, and the biggest challenge they mention is the time it takes to manage notifications constantly. Fortunately, most apps offer integrations with other productivity tools to help you quickly minimize notifications. You can automate repetitive tasks or reminders. If you don't want to keep the "Do Not Disturb" mode always on like I do. For example, you can set your apps to automatically switch to "Do Not Disturb" when a meeting starts or use apps like Zapier to help you create an automation that doesn't exist. This way, you spend less time managing distractions and more time focusing on essential tasks, all without feeling overwhelmed or missing out on what truly matters. Leverage tools like Microsoft's "Do not Disturb" feature, Sunsama's focus mode or Google's "Focus Time" to block out periods dedicated solely to deep work.

Consider automating simple tasks like booking meetings to stay focused and avoid the endless back-and-forth of scheduling emails. Instead of asking, "What time works for you?" and waiting for a reply, send a personalized calendar link where others can choose a time that works for them.

Also, use AI to draft emails, summarize meeting notes, or auto-tag documents for easier search later.

✦ PRO TIP: When working on essential tasks, automate switching your apps to full-screen mode to eliminate distractions from other windows, notifications, and the temptation to multitask, allowing you to stay focused on what matters.

Focus and ADHD: Extra tips

When you are neurodiverse or suffer from ADD or ADHD, Attention-Deficit / Hyperactivity Disorder, or any other neurodevelopmental disorder that makes it more challenging to focus, some of these tips may work but may not be enough. Here are some more specialized tips. As I am not a doctor or psychologist specializing in ADHD, these tips are not a cure or medical advice, but they won't hurt to try as a way to deal with ADHD in the day-to-day. While the reasons for lack of focus may vary from person to person, I have seen how many coachees with ADHD also implement the same principle I share in the book, showing remarkable results.

If you don't have ADHD, you may realize other coworkers or direct reports do have to deal with it and empathize with them. Understand their different needs, ask how you can support them, and find ways to enjoy daily tasks together by looking for a common purpose or a long-term goal that keeps them excited. Approximately 15-20% of people are neurodiverse, which means at least one in ten of your coworkers may be part of this group. It is crucial to understand and appreciate their unique strengths, as well as the challenges they may face.

What is ADHD

ADHD is a neurodevelopmental disorder[xvii] characterized by hyperactivity, inattention, and impulsivity. The person finds it hard to focus. Despite *really* wanting to tackle a task, you find yourself unable to begin and maybe even experience a sense of paralysis. Your brain has two networks, DMN and TPN, which should work one at a time, while when you have ADHD, they both work at the same time, trying to daydream and focus at the same time.

Not everyone who has trouble focusing has ADHD, and it is not true that people with ADHD cannot focus at all.

Multitasking is one of the strengths that individuals with ADHD can excel at, which can benefit both them and their employers. The ability to multitask often fosters creativity and innovation. Individuals with ADHD may excel at connecting disparate ideas and finding unconventional solutions to complex problems. They can also quickly adjust their focus and priorities based on changing demands and priorities. When they do find a task they enjoy, they can become hyperfocused and work for hours, losing track of time.

Multitasking with compassion: Pairing Tasks

People with hyperactivity or ADHD often find it challenging to concentrate on a single task for extended periods as their brain works differently. The urge to engage in other activities—such as watching TV, singing, or fidgeting—while trying to focus on work or reading is common. While this may feel distracting sometimes, it's perfectly normal and can even be leveraged to enhance productivity.

Whether or not you have ADHD, instead of resisting these impulses, try embracing them! If engaging in a secondary activity helps you stay focused on your primary task, use it to your advantage. This approach essentially "tricks" your brain, which craves novelty and stimulation, by allowing it to switch between different activities while maintaining focus.

For example, you could alternate between working on a project and reading a book or between painting and writing an email. Writing while listening to music or keeping a fidget toy nearby during study sessions helps you concentrate better. The key is to choose two relatively small tasks that aren't related to each other. One of them, like fidgeting or listening to music, should not require much mental effort, so it doesn't interfere with your primary task. This way, you can either do them simultaneously or switch back and forth between activities without losing your train of thought.

By embracing this multitasking method, you can use your natural tendency for novelty and stimulation to stay engaged and productive without feeling overwhelmed. It's about finding the right balance and allowing your brain the flexibility it needs to stay focused on the work that matters.

✦ PRO TIP: Group and Cut Into Halves

Individuals with ADHD tend to prefer dealing with smaller tasks to avoid getting overwhelmed. To make things easier, you can group similar tasks together and then divide them into smaller chunks that can be completed within 25 minutes. If a task seems too big to handle, you can split it into two halves. Additionally, you can multitask by working on two tasks from the same group simultaneously.

Manage Your Environment

Identify where you can focus more. Is it at home, at work or at a Starbucks? See if this is an accommodation you can request. ADHDers are more sensitive to their environment, so controlling what you hear and what's around you is essential. By doing so, you can minimize distractions and improve your focus. Check the 5S method in the next chapter to learn more about how to keep your environment organized or read my book 5S Your Life.

Emotional Shifts to Cultivate Focus with Compassion

As you have seen, focus is choosing where to direct your energy and eliminating distractions. However, many struggle with guilt when they can't do it all. This is where self-compassion becomes critical—acknowledging that you're human, not a machine, and progress begins with realistic expectations.

Compassion in focus means recognizing your limits and avoiding overloading your to-do list. Improving your focus can be a matter of habits and self-awareness.

Overcoming the Fear of Starting

The fear of starting a task can be paralyzing, especially when it feels overwhelming or unfamiliar. One way to overcome this fear is to break the task down into smaller, more manageable steps, as we discussed before.

A helpful approach is to ask yourself, "What's the worst that can happen if I start this?" Consider the worst-case scenario, such as not knowing exactly what to say or making a mistake. The reality is that most tasks don't require perfection—they require progress. The fear of failure often holds you back, but by reminding yourself that mistakes are part of the process, you can shift your mindset and take that first step. If you don't know where to start, you may need to overcome your analysis paralysis.

Overcoming Analysis Paralysis

Decision-making paralysis occurs when you're overwhelmed by too many choices or the fear of making the wrong decision. It often leads to inaction as you struggle to pick the best option. To break free from this, simplifying the decision-making process is key. One way to do this is by reducing the number of decisions you need to make daily.

For instance, Steve Jobs and Mark Zuckerberg are known for reducing decision fatigue by wearing the same type of clothing every day. By eliminating the need to decide what to wear, they preserve their mental energy for more important decisions. Similarly, I choose my clothes and schedule my calendar the night before. This practice helps me avoid decision paralysis the next day when my brain is still warming up and not ready to make quick decisions.

However, if your decision-making process needs to be more complex or the decision is crucial, you can use more precise decision-making models to help structure your approach. For example, tools like AMFE (Failure Mode and Effects Analysis) or other decision frameworks can help you analyze the potential risks and outcomes, ensuring that your decision is well-informed and thoughtfully considered.

A straightforward way to move forward is to practice triage, a decision-making approach borrowed from emergencies. When you don't have all the information to decide, commit at least one action to move forward. Instead of waiting for perfect clarity, take an initial action to create momentum, breaking the most urgent and important tasks into manageable steps and adjusting as new information arises. Start with what you already know, ask someone, or research more (yes, that is also moving forward). Your goal is to get moving.

If aspects of the decision are out of your control, don't hesitate to ask for help. Reaching out to others for their insights can provide clarity and offer a fresh perspective.

I was recently coaching someone with ADHD, and we were having trouble making progress. We discussed many options, but she struggled to implement them, and we kept circling back to square one. I asked what else she needed, and she explained that she wanted to implement the strategies together—experimenting firsthand, such as using the Eisenhower Matrix with her actual backlog. This way, she could better understand and follow the steps. She asked if I could "hold her hand" through the process, and of course, I was happy to support her in this way. It may seem simple now, but it took us some time to uncover precisely what she needed to move forward, and that is OK! Take the time you need.

✦ PRO TIP: Lastly, embrace the Lean Startup mindset: **try small and fail fast**. Rather than seeing decisions as irreversible, view them as opportunities for learning and growth. Mistakes are simply part of the process, and quick iterations allow you to adjust and improve without getting bogged down in fear of failure. This mindset encourages experimentation and flexibility, allowing you to take action without being paralyzed by perfectionism (we will discuss this more in detail in the Finish chapter).

By simplifying everyday choices, using structured decision-making models when necessary, asking for help, and embracing trial and error, you can overcome decision paralysis and make more confident, practical choices.

One of my coachees was struggling with starting tasks, particularly when it came to responding to emails. She felt overwhelmed by the decision-making process—deciding what to do, how to do it, and where to start. Together, we worked to break down her challenge and approach it step by step:

- **Identify the Root Cause**: We identified that the most challenging part for her was simply getting started. She feared making the wrong decision and felt overwhelmed by the task itself.
- **Breaking it Down**: I encouraged her to commit to 30-minute focused time. The goal was not perfection but just to start and make progress, even if the task wasn't completed immediately.
- **Avoiding Distractions**: To eliminate distractions, we set up strategies like turning off her phone's Do Not Disturb feature and closing unnecessary tabs on her computer, allowing her to focus solely on the task.
- **Self-Reminders**: We created a list of simple reminders to keep her on track when she felt stuck, such as asking, "What can I control right now?" or "What small step can I take to make progress?"
- **Worst-case scenario**: We also discussed the worst-case scenario for responding to the emails. "What's the worst that can happen? You might not know what to say. You might not say it perfectly. Can you ask for help? What happens if it's not perfect?" It helped her reframe the task and take the pressure off herself.
- **Celebrating Success**: She agreed she would try to recognize her effort at the end of the day and felt proud of how she had managed the task. She recognized that perfection wasn't the goal—progress was.

By breaking the task into smaller, more manageable steps and addressing her fears with self-compassion, she overcame procrastination and felt more confident in tackling similar challenges in the future.

Through this compassionate and structured approach, she learned to face her fears, manage her time more effectively, and celebrate her progress—without the pressure of perfection.

Prioritizing Yourself Over Pleasing Others

*"I try to be everything to everyone
all the time; I am a people pleaser."*

This statement is often heard from those who struggle with managing their priorities. It's challenging to decide what to focus on first or stick to your own schedule when you feel like other people's needs are more important. A key shift in your time management toward achieving well-being involves accepting that you can't do everything for everyone. Constantly prioritizing others' needs means neglecting your own. While it's essential to be attuned to the needs of others, it's equally important to express your own needs and prioritize what matters most to you—without shame or guilt. If you don't prioritize your well-being, who will? Here are some things to consider:

Setting Boundaries with Compassion

One of the first shifts in mastering time management with compassion is learning how to set boundaries—both with others and with yourself. Establishing clear limits while remaining kind to others and yourself is important. Saying "no" doesn't have to come with guilt or defensiveness; it's an act of self-respect and a vital step in protecting your energy. By setting boundaries, you create space for what truly matters. Start by prioritizing the two most important tasks for today— your *20% vital few* that will drive the greatest impact before saying yes to other responsibilities. Once those are completed, remain flexible and open to supporting others with the rest of your time.

Understand Your Core Values

Knowing your core values is essential for prioritizing your needs with intention. When you align your activities with your values and your *North Star* (more on this in Chapter *Flow*), decision-making becomes clearer and more fulfilling. Instead of feeling pulled in multiple directions, you'll naturally gravitate toward what truly matters. This clarity empowers you to let go of distractions and external demands that don't serve your personal or professional goals. Take time to reflect on your values and use them as a guiding compass for managing your time, energy, and focus.

Prioritize Self-Care

Prioritizing self-care is not selfish—it's essential for maintaining a healthy balance in your life. When you make time for yourself, you replenish your energy, allowing you to show up as your best self for others. Self-care should be an intentional part of your schedule, just like any other important task. Whether it's taking time to rest, pursuing a hobby, or simply enjoying quiet moments for reflection, self-care is crucial. Treat it as a non-negotiable priority within your time management strategy. I'll dive deeper into self-care in the following chapters, particularly in Chapter 8, where we explore the role of Compassion.

"By focusing on just two priorities at a time, I was able to make meaningful progress and unlock real opportunities in both areas."

Takeaways

- **Check Email Time**: Dedicated periods for managing emails instead of constantly checking throughout the day.
- **4Ds:** A time-management strategy to help prioritize tasks: **Do Now**, **Do Later, Delegate**, and **Delete**.
- **Eisenhower Matrix**: A decision-making tool that categorizes tasks based on urgency and importance to help prioritize effectively.
- **3D a task:** delegate, defer or delete the task.
- **Time Fragmentation**: The "switching time" required to concentrate on a task after an interruption reduces productivity and interrupts flow. It takes at least 15 minutes to become productive again after a distraction.
- **Do Now Tasks**: Tasks that align with your long-term goals and can push your career or projects forward meaningfully.
- **ADHD (Attention Deficit Hyperactivity Disorder)**: A neurodevelopmental condition that can affect focus, attention, and time management. People with ADHD often benefit from structured time management strategies, like timeboxing, to improve productivity.
- **Batching Email by Natural Interruption**: A method of checking emails during natural breaks in your workflow, such as between tasks or meetings, rather than constantly checking throughout the day. It reduces distractions and improves focus.
- **Pareto Principle Applied to Time Management**: Also known as the 80/20 rule, suggests that 80% of your results come from 20% of your efforts. You can maximize your productivity and time efficiency by identifying and focusing on the most impactful tasks.

- **People-Pleasing:** The tendency to prioritize others' needs over your own, often leading to neglect of personal wellbeing and overextension.

Practical Tips to Cultivate Compassionate Focus TODAY

Morning Check-In
Begin each day with a simple but powerful question: "What's most important to me today?" Identifying 1-2 non-negotiable tasks that align with your long-term goals helps you focus on what truly matters and sets a clear intention for the day ahead.

Limit Multi-tasking
Commit to focusing on one task at a time. While multitasking may seem efficient, it often reduces the quality of your work and increases stress. Break tasks into manageable chunks and create a distraction-free environment to make focusing on one thing at a time more manageable.

Practice Self-Compassion
If distractions or setbacks arise, approach them with kindness. Instead of criticizing yourself, gently guide your focus back to the task, telling yourself it is OK. This compassionate approach helps maintain a positive mindset and fosters a sustainable, productive flow throughout the day.

Download the worksheet for this chapter at
www.lucypaulise.com/timebox

Chapter 6 | FLOW
Enjoy The Task At Hand

How can you make your tasks enjoyable and enter a flow state where productivity and creativity peak?

"I no longer can dedicate time to the things I enjoy doing at work, like coding, because I never have the time. I have so much on my plate that I get distracted by the most urgent thing to do."

Flow[xviii] is that magical mental state where you're fully immersed in a task, experiencing energy, focus, and engagement all at once. It's the sweet spot where productivity and satisfaction converge, allowing you to perform at your highest potential. But reaching this state is not as simple as crossing off tasks from your to-do list. Achieving flow requires a careful balance of mindset, emotional state, and environment.

In the previous chapter, we explored how to be able to focus. If you focus long enough, you can taste the sweetness of the state of flow—what Mihaly Csikszentmihalyi[xix] calls an "optimal experience." When you can concentrate deeply, the quality of your work improves, and the joy you get from accomplishing your task increases. It's about connecting your attention with your energy and allowing both to sync with the task.

Remember when you were so immersed in something you loved that hours seemed to vanish? That's the power of flow. Whether coding, writing, or working on a passion project, being in a flow state can transform your work into a productive and fulfilling experience. In this chapter, we'll explore how you can cultivate flow in your work, making every task more enjoyable and effortlessly productive.

I remember entering a state of flow when I was a roller skater. During my 3-minute routines, I sometimes performed flawlessly, even exceeding my usual abilities. I'd jump higher, and my legs would stretch further, feeling almost superhuman. As a young teen, I didn't fully understand how it worked. I could not perform always the same way, and more significantly, I could not always perform this way, but when I did, it was a fantastic feeling. It was like flying with my skates on, enjoying the moment, and achieving my best result.

One competition, while I was deeply immersed in the flow state and performing exceptionally, a stray thought entered my mind: "I'm doing great; I'm going to win this!" The distraction broke my concentration, and I immediately stumbled on the next move. Thinking about the future had disrupted my flow state.

The Lack of Motivation

Time management is not just about processes and discipline; it's also about your emotional state and being motivated. While having the right tools and techniques is essential, the ability to manage your time effectively hinges on your mental and emotional wellbeing. Even the best time management systems can fall apart if you are stressed, anxious, or unmotivated.

One of the biggest obstacles to managing time effectively is the inability to enjoy the task at hand. Worrying about the past or feeling anxious about the future can negatively impact productivity. Your brain focuses more on avoiding stress and preventing a disastrous potential outcome than on taking the following steps to grow.

Hector Garcia and Francesc Miralles, in their book *Ikigai: the Japanese Secret to a Long Happy Life*[xx], state that "To achieve this optimal experience, we have to focus on increasing the time we spend on activities that bring us to this state of flow, rather than allowing ourselves to get caught up in activities that offer immediate pleasure— like overeating, abusing drugs or alcohol, or stuffing ourselves with chocolate in front of the TV."

The Power of Flow

In his national bestseller book Flow, Mihaly Csikszentmihalyi explains how it works. Neither boredom nor anxiety are positive experiences. Instead, the optimal experience is finding the ideal state where people can enjoy their work, feel productive, immerse themselves in what they are doing, and perform at their best.

People usually find it easier to get into flow when doing something they enjoy and are good at, such as making music, rock climbing, dancing, sailing, or playing chess.

Employees can also look for ways to achieve flow at work.

Mihaly explains, "Flow is not the same for everyone, even doing the same activities. How we feel at any given moment of a flow activity is strongly influenced by the objective conditions; some patterns are enjoyable, but whether we enjoy or not is ultimately up to us."

This pleasurable experience makes work feel less like work and significantly boosts productivity and creativity. When you're in a flow state, you can accomplish tasks more efficiently and with higher-quality results.

The precise hormonal changes during the flow state are still under investigation, but research suggests that it involves a combination of increased dopamine, norepinephrine, endorphins, serotonin, and anandamide. These neurochemicals work together to create feelings of pleasure, focus, motivation, and wellbeing, characteristic of the flow experience.

- Dopamine: Plays a key role in motivation, reward, and focus.
- Norepinephrine: Increases arousal, attention, and energy levels.
- Endorphins: Natural painkillers that promote feelings of euphoria and wellbeing.
- Serotonin: Contributes to feelings of happiness, satisfaction, and overall mood regulation.

The enjoyment you derive from flow creates a positive feedback loop, motivating you to repeat the behaviors and routines that led to it. Consistent repetition makes these routines ingrained, requiring minimal effort and conscious thought. Automating routine tasks frees up mental energy for more complex and creative endeavors.

The benefits of flow extend beyond individual performance. It can lead to several benefits, including:

- **Increased Productivity and Efficiency:** Flow allows for deep concentration and complete immersion in the task, leading to higher output and better quality work in less time.
- **Enhanced Creativity and Innovation:** The flow state fosters a heightened sense of creativity, enabling individuals and teams to generate more innovative ideas and solutions.
- **Improved Job Satisfaction and Wellbeing:** Flow is a pleasurable experience that leads to increased job satisfaction, reduced stress, and greater fulfillment in one's work.
- **Stronger Team Collaboration and Performance:** When team members experience flow together, it can improve communication, coordination, and overall team performance.

The ultimate goal is to integrate flow into your daily routine so thoroughly that it becomes your default mode of operation. If you have at least one or two blocks of time in your day involving flow, you can transform your brain chemicals to work in your favor.

By effortlessly achieving and maintaining this state, you can consistently perform at your best and experience greater satisfaction and success in your work and personal life.

Common reasons people struggle to get into the Flow State:

- Unclear goals: Without a clear direction, you may struggle to know where to begin or what to prioritize.

- Distracting environment: Frequent interruptions, noise, and notifications prevent deep, uninterrupted focus.
- Mismatch in challenge level: Tasks that are too easy cause boredom, while overly difficult ones lead to frustration, making it hard to stay engaged.
- Stress, anxiety, or lack of connection: Feeling overwhelmed, anxious, or unmotivated because a task is irrelevant or meaningless can hinder the flow experience.

Question for you
What are your primary triggers for losing your flow state?
Can you prioritize them so that you have your primary triggers at the top?

Common Challenges of the Flow State: Procrastination and Workaholism

While entering a state of flow can be incredibly rewarding, it's not always smooth sailing. Two common challenges are procrastination and *hyperflow*. Procrastination occurs when you avoid starting a task altogether, often due to being overwhelmed or afraid. *Hyperflow*, however, is the opposite: it happens when you're so deeply immersed in a task that you lose track of time and cannot step back, take breaks, or switch tasks when necessary.

Challenge #1: Procrastination

If you tend to be a procrastinator, when you feel stressed or overwhelmed, you will try to avoid dealing with a crucial task by working on less critical tasks or getting distracted, for example, by spending time on social media.

You are confident about your abilities, so you might convince yourself that you'll come back to the important task later, but when you do start, you might only tackle the more manageable parts and procrastinate on the challenging aspects or hyperfocus only working on the tasks you enjoy, working extra hours but not getting all the job done. This tendency to avoid critical and urgent tasks can lead to poor planning, increased stress and mental and physical exhaustion, resulting in completing the task late or at the last minute and undermining your self-care.

Many people I talk to confess they "work better under stress." In most cases, the deadline stress helps them focus; it is as if they don't have time to overthink. While this can be true, working under stress is not healthy in the long term, as your body can only work effectively under stress for a limited period, and then, it gets burned out. As adrenaline kicks in, people feel like they are enjoying the moment, but the reality is that working under stress doesn't get people to enjoy what they are doing; they are simply trying to get it out of their way. Procrastination is a way to avoid stressful situations, but ultimately, it's only delaying it.

Coping mechanism: When procrastinating, you struggle to enter the flow state. Intimidated by large or complex tasks, you put them off until the pressure becomes overwhelming. Avoid challenges or tasks you don't enjoy by "escaping" or deferring them.

Challenge #2: Workaholism and Hyperflow

While flow is about maintaining a healthy balance of focus and flexibility, hyperflow can lead to overwork. Sometimes, it can cause you to lose track of time, as if you were in a trance, doing non-essential tasks or getting too involved in the details. Hyperflow is especially common when you're highly engaged in something and feel that the task demands your complete attention. However, this deep immersion can result in burnout or neglecting other important aspects of your life or work.

While flow is productive and sustainable, *hyperflow* can become challenging when it prevents you from managing your energy, transitioning between tasks, or maintaining balance. It is very common, particularly for individuals with ADHD.

If unchecked, you may spiral into *workaholism*. You become so absorbed in what you're doing that you lose track of time, pushing well beyond healthy limits. Workaholism is rooted in a need to do more, working excessively without necessarily aiming for perfection, which we will discuss in the next chapter. It's about effort and volume, often without considering whether the work is effective or meaningful.

- Example: Staying up all night to work on multiple projects, even if some are unnecessary or could be delegated.

While being immersed in a state of flow can be beneficial, continuously overstaying there can lead to exhaustion, burnout, and diminished returns.

Coping mechanism: immersing yourself only in tasks you enjoy.

Ultimately, the goal is to find a comfortable balance— staying in flow for a limited, intentional period— helping yourself enter a manageable flow state, neither overstaying as a workaholic nor failing to arrive as a procrastinator.

Question for you
How would you rate your ability to enter the flow state, from 1 (I am in the state of flow maybe once a week) to 10 (I usually get into the state of flow one, twice or more times a day)?

Behavioral Shifts To Achieving Flow State

This chapter will guide you through the essentials of achieving flow by focusing on the interplay between your emotional state and time management practices. You will learn how to create an environment conducive to deep work, harness your motivation, and maintain a positive mindset. By addressing time management's practical and emotional aspects, you can navigate your tasks quickly and efficiently, ultimately leading to a more fulfilling and productive work life.

We will explore techniques for minimizing distractions, setting clear goals, and maintaining a sense of purpose in your work. You will also discover strategies for staying motivated, even when faced with mundane or boring tasks. Remember, managing your time effectively is not just about ticking off tasks on your list but about finding joy and satisfaction in the process.

With some tweaks to your routine, you can make the most of this time and even get ahead and overcome procrastination and workaholism, no matter how easy or complicated the task ahead.

Let's dive into the journey of achieving flow and unlock the full potential of your timeboxing practice, ensuring that you get things done and feel great while doing it.

How to Achieve an Optimal Experience

According to Mihaly Csikszentmihalyi, the essential steps in this process to achieve an optimal experience are:

Set an achievable but challenging goal

As we reviewed in the last chapter, setting at least one challenging goal each day to accomplish during your scheduled time can be helpful. If your goal seems too daunting, it's easy to procrastinate. Break it into smaller, realistically achievable sub-goals when goals or tasks feel overwhelming. The goal you want to achieve should be challenging but not so complex that it scares you. If it's too easy, you might get bored and find it hard to get into a state of flow.

For instance, instead of aiming to call 50 clients a day to meet a quota, which may seem intimidating, try to achieve your flow by aiming to call just five clients in 30-minute chunks. This approach makes the task "appear" more achievable and less overwhelming.

Find ways of measuring progress

Tracking your progress is crucial to maintain motivation and a sense of accomplishment. Make sure your goals can be measured. Just like a climber conquering a challenging peak or a dancer mastering a complex choreography, achieving each step of the way provides a tangible sense of advancement. Whether coding a software program or writing a book, visualizing your progress and recognizing how each completed task brings you closer to the final objective can be incredibly motivating. For instance, aim to code one feature or write ten pages daily. This helps you stay on track and prevents you from feeling overwhelmed by the magnitude of the project ahead.

Stay present

Stay present and fully immersed in the task at hand. It's easy to get sidetracked by thoughts about the end result, potential criticisms, or the looming workload. However, these distractions can fuel anxiety and hinder your progress. By anchoring your attention to the present moment and the specific activity you're engaged in, you can quiet your mind, reduce stress, and enter a flow state. You can use mindful breathing, which I will describe later, to help you stay present.

Develop the skills necessary

To stay in flow, it's essential to continuously develop and refine the skills required to excel in tasks that bring you joy. Mastering new techniques boosts your competence and keeps you engaged and motivated. By committing to lifelong learning, you ensure that the challenges you face remain stimulating, allowing you to deepen your expertise and sustain your passion for the work you do.

Whether taking a course, seeking feedback, or practicing regularly, actively cultivating the skills necessary for your passions will keep you in a flow state and drive you toward more success.

Achieving flow may be difficult if the activity feels consistently challenging, even when broken into smaller steps. Keep pushing forward. With consistent practice, seeking additional knowledge or resources, and asking for help, you can gradually close the gap between your current abilities and the task's demands.

✦ PRO TIP: Remember, reaching out to colleagues, mentors, or supervisors for guidance or support is perfectly fine.

Over time, as you build the necessary skills and confidence, the task will become more manageable, and the flow state will become more accessible. The key is to embrace the learning process, not just the end result. Be patient with yourself, enjoy the journey, and celebrate your progress along the way. When you love what you're doing and take joy in your work, time seems to fade away.

Keep Raising The Stakes

If the activity becomes too easy or repetitive, explore ways to increase its complexity and challenge yourself. It could involve taking on additional responsibilities, setting more ambitious goals, or learning new skills that take you to the next level, allowing you to approach the task from a fresh perspective.

"The key is always having a meaningful challenge to overcome," say Hector Garcia and Francesc Miralles. As you continue to improve and master your current tasks, seeking out new challenges will be essential to maintaining a flow state and preventing boredom. Don't hesitate to discuss these opportunities with your manager, as they may be able to suggest ways to expand your role or provide you with more stimulating projects.

Getting in the Flow Through Rituals

Out of the five rules for achieving the flow state, the one that I find the most difficult is to stay present on what you are doing instead of getting anxious.

When I was a figure skater, I couldn't tell how I knew or what made me figure out that this could help me, but I also had a ritual for every competition. I would wear the same clothes, eat the same food the night before, and bring a puppy toy on the day of the event and use the same perfume and hair spray. Similarly, a famous tennis player, Rafael Nadal, has a pre-serve ritual of complex twitches and ticks. In his 2011 book titled "Rafa: My Story,"[xxi] he explained that it helps him to get into the right mindset for a match: "It is a way of placing myself in a match, of ordering my environment to match the order I am looking for in my head." The Olympic swimmer Michael Phelps also reported following strict rituals for the 210 minutes before any race. And finally, the Haka performed by New Zealand's rugby team is another example of a ritual utilized in sports.

Rituals consist of a rigid sequence of behaviors often performed in the same order. They provide a structured framework, a "process within the chaos" that can help you navigate the uncertainties of their professional journeys.

In his book Chatter[xxii], Ethan Kross explores various strategies for managing the inner voice that contributes to anxiety, stress and negativity, and he also suggests incorporating rituals into your workday to increase your sense of control.

Imagine using rituals the same way athletes do—**as a powerful tool to enhance focus, boost confidence, and reduce stress** in high-pressure situations. Rituals can be your **secret weapon** for conquering workplace anxiety, improving productivity, and achieving a state of flow.

For example, consider preparing for an important meeting. Instead of feeling overwhelmed, you can break it down into structured steps, creating a ritual that builds confidence and minimizes uncertainty:

- **A week before:** Review key points, anticipate questions, and refine your message.
- **30 minutes before:** Run through your main talking points, visualize success, and ensure your environment is distraction-free.
- **Right before the meeting:** Take **two minutes of deep breathing** doing Amy Cuddy's power pose[xxiii] to calm your nerves and boost confidence.
- Wear a go-to outfit that makes you feel strong, log into Zoom **exactly five minutes early**, or review notes one last time.
- **After the meeting:** Reflect on what went well and jot down takeaways for future improvement.

These small, intentional habits help shift your mindset from nervousness to readiness. When repeated consistently, rituals become automatic confidence boosters, helping you show up as your best self, time and time again.

Establishing a morning routine like I suggested in the Timeboxing chapter or a pre-work ritual can create a sense of control and stability, counteracting the chaos that often accompanies career challenges.

Kross suggests that rituals psychologically affect individuals by grounding them in the present moment and reducing the impact of stressful situations. Rituals can positively influence performance in high-pressure situations by providing a sense of order and control.

Rituals impact our brains, reducing cortisol levels and promoting a sense of calm, making people feel less anxious and having a lower heart rate. By understanding the science behind the practice, why not use it in the workplace to improve your performance during meetings and presentations?

One such ritual that is commonly used in manufacturing is cleaning. I have explained this in detail in my book *5S Your Life*[xxiv]. By cleaning and organizing your workstation in a standardized way before or after your shift, you can reduce distractions and second-guessing and keep your mind clear to enter the state of flow more easily throughout your shift. This ritual can be applied to any workstation or home office by ensuring that nothing is on your desk except your computer and water bottle before you start your day.

You can also convert your 15-minute planning routine into a ritual by doing it always at the same time, using the same apps, drinking the same cup of coffee and turning on the same song.

Small actions and habits can have a big impact on our mental wellbeing, particularly in professional settings where anxiety can be prevalent. Whether it's a simple ritual before a big meeting or to help wind down after work, these practices can create a positive ripple effect on our overall wellbeing. By embracing and personalizing these rituals, we can cultivate a calmer mindset and ultimately thrive in our careers.

Stay Present with Breathing

A practice that has helped me avoid going into a rabbit hole with negative thoughts is breathing. Breathing training helps us direct attention to where we want to focus instead of leaving our brain to control us. Richard Boyatzis, in his book *Helping People Change*[xxv], confirms that the antidote to stressful experiences is doing renewal activities, such as exercise, meditation, even playing with your kids, or mindfulness throughout your day.

Training the mind can make it easier to enter a state of flow, and meditation or mindfulness are powerful tools for strengthening our mental faculties. The goal is to calm your mind, observe your thoughts and emotions, and focus your attention on a single point. The basic practice involves sitting upright and concentrating on your breath. This practice generates alpha and theta brain waves, the same ones activated just before we fall asleep or after a relaxing hot bath. The key is that you don't need to be in a hot tub to feel relaxed—you can achieve this sense of calm at any time simply by observing your breath.

Dr. Amishi Jha[xxvi], neuroscientist and director of the Mindfulness Research and Practice Initiative at the University of Miami, explains, "Wherever attention goes, the rest of the brain follows. Where you pay attention shapes your life's experience."

When anxiety strikes, our minds often dwell on past mistakes, future worries, or tasks we still need to accomplish. This cycle of negative thinking distracts us from the present, adding stress. What's more, as leaders, our moods are contagious, affecting those around us—positively or negatively.

Managing our breath offers a solution by helping us direct our attention rather than letting our minds control us. Richard Boyatzis, in *Helping People Change*, emphasizes that activities like exercise, meditation, and mindfulness act as antidotes to stress.

Mindfulness of breathing is a focused-attention practice that, like a workout, can be strengthened with regular practice. Here's how to do it:

1. **Sit upright**: Pay attention to your breathing and feel your abdomen rising and falling.
2. **Notice what arises in your mind**: Think of 3 positive things, like achievements or moments of pride.
3. **Return your focus to the breath**: When your mind wanders, gently redirect your attention back to your breath.

You will improve attention over time by practicing this for 10-20 minutes daily, or at least 2 minutes right before that call that you are so worried about.

Add Purpose To Each Task

When faced with a challenging, overwhelming, monotonous, boring task, procrastination often creeps in, and you will avoid it at all costs.

Define the purpose of the task before starting. What does that task mean to you? How will it help you succeed? What makes it essential to finish it? How can you use your strengths to do it?

If you still don't find meaning in this task after asking yourself all these questions, you may discover that you should not be doing it at all (remember the 4D: maybe it is not a Do Now task, but a Do Later, Delegate, or Delete). As long as it is a Do, there should be a purpose attached to it. Find it and remind yourself of it if, at any time during your timebox, you want to stop doing it or postpone it. Write the purpose of that task on a piece of paper or Post-it if it helps you, or directly on your calendar timebox.

When I recommended this, many people said, "Well, I cannot say no to this client or that request from my manager." Still, you can ask yourself, how does that task help you achieve your goals? You may need to do it to accomplish a bigger task, such as getting the desired promotion. It also helps you learn a new skill or support that teammate who helped you out yesterday. Open your perspective, and you will see how it is all connected.

The 10-Minute Rule for Managing Distractions

As we reviewed in the Focus chapter, one of the biggest challenges to maintaining flow is the constant urge to check your phone, browse social media, or engage in other distractions. When discussing flow, once we overcome distractions, the key is to explore how to sustain uninterrupted work once focus is achieved.

The 10-Minute Rule is a simple yet effective strategy to help you sustain focus and remain in a flow state. While the 5-Minute Rule encourages you to start a task by committing to just five minutes of effort, the 10-Minute Rule helps you resist distractions and stay on track once you've started working. The idea is to wait at least 10 more minutes before switching to another task or giving in to a distraction.

This technique is handy during your power time—when you're most productive and focused. Instead of immediately responding to an impulse to check your phone, answer emails, or switch tasks, you commit to continuing your current task for 10 more minutes. This brief delay allows your brain to push past fleeting urges, making it easier to maintain deep focus and complete high-priority work efficiently. Over time, this practice strengthens your ability to stay engaged, reducing multitasking and improving overall productivity.

The 10-Minute Rule works like this: When you feel the urge to do something distracting, tell yourself to wait 10 minutes. This rule creates a slight, manageable delay that helps you resist the temptation to give in to distractions immediately. Often, by the time those 10 minutes have passed, the urge to check your phone or divert your attention has subsided, and you can return to your task with renewed focus.

The beauty of the 10-Minute Rule lies in its simplicity. Instead of trying to fight off distractions by force, you're simply postponing them for a short time. This can be a surprisingly effective strategy because distractions often feel urgent, but when you delay them, you realize they aren't as pressing as they initially seemed. Giving yourself a brief window of time to continue focusing on your work helps you break the cycle of giving in to distractions every time they arise.

Using this rule, you train your mind to tolerate those urges without acting on them immediately. This builds your self-discipline and strengthens your ability to focus for extended periods. Over time, you'll notice that your tolerance for distractions increases, and you become more adept at staying focused for longer periods.

✦ PRO TIP: How to Use the 10-Minute Rule to Stay in the Flow state:

1. **Pause and Acknowledge**: When you feel the urge to check your phone or engage in distracting behavior, pause and acknowledge the urge without giving in.

2. **Commit to Waiting**: Tell yourself, "I will wait 10 minutes before giving in to this distraction." The simple act of setting a timer or making a mental commitment helps reinforce your self-control.

3. **Focus on the Task at Hand**: During these 10 minutes, redirect your attention back to your task. You'll often find that the urge to distract yourself fades away as you engage more deeply in your work.

4. **Reevaluate After 10 Minutes**: After the 10-minute delay, ask yourself if the distraction is still necessary. You'll often realize that you don't need to act on the urge at all and can stay focused.

The power of the 10-Minute Rule comes from the way it shifts your relationship with distractions. Distractions are often most appealing because they offer an immediate, quick escape from the work at hand. However, by delaying this immediate gratification for just 10 minutes, you break the habit of giving in to these distractions and create a mental barrier that helps you stay focused longer.

This technique works well because 10 minutes is short enough to feel manageable but long enough to allow the initial urge to fade. It teaches you that not every distraction needs to be acted upon immediately and that you can regain control of your focus.

Schedule Breaks

As recommended in the previous chapters, it is not only OK to schedule regular breaks but also essential for preventing burnout. Schedule specific times for lunch and exercise to rest your brain and keep your energy levels up, especially after experiencing a period of flow. For instance, if I want to have a deep and long writing session, I make sure it is between my breakfast and lunch or between my lunch and coffee time around 3 pm. If I only have a few hours to focus, I make it right after breakfast. If, as I said before, I don't have time during the day to stay in flow for a long period, I wake up a little earlier, like at 6, with no breakfast, and just go straight to work until 7, so it is a short period, but you get to be in hyperf-flow. I may accomplish even more in this hour than 2 hours later when distractions and new urgent tasks abound.

Step away from your desk to enjoy your meal or incorporate physical activity into your day, whether a quick walk, a yoga session, or a workout at the gym. Exercise boosts your mood, increases energy levels, improves cognitive function, and enhances productivity, increasing the odds of having one or more flow sessions during the day.

Keep a Distraction Journal

Keeping a distraction journal can be a helpful strategy if you find it challenging to concentrate while working. Even when there are no external distractions—such as audible or visual interruptions, as discussed in the *Focus* chapter—

internal distractions can still disrupt your concentration, which is the central challenge addressed in this *Flow* chapter. Your mind might wander to unrelated tasks, reminders, or random thoughts. Whenever this happens, jot down whatever is pulling your attention away. This simple act lets you acknowledge the distraction without letting it derail your progress, helping you maintain momentum and refocus more effectively.

Keep your journal or a backlog handy to make capturing these thoughts easier. I have Post-its on my desk for quick notes when an idea strikes, especially during a call or meeting. I also keep a journal on my nightstand for those moments when I can't sleep, often because an idea is buzzing around in my mind. Writing it down helps clear my head, relax, and return to sleep more easily.

You can use digital tools like Google Keep or Google Tasks on your phone or simply grab a traditional notebook. The key is having a reliable spot to quickly jot down these distractions, freeing your mind to refocus on the task at hand. Later, you can revisit your journal to deal with these thoughts at a more appropriate time. This simple practice helps you regain control of your attention and stay productive.

Create a dedicated to-do list that is easy to access and update from your phone, tablet and laptop. By the end of the day, you can review it, evaluate priorities, celebrate and plan for the following day.

Set a Timer

When timeboxing, the goal is to spend a certain amount of time on each task. But, when you are in hyper-flow status, your brain can get so immersed that you lose track of time and may not even see the notification to start the next task. While it is excellent to hyperfocus, sometimes it can make you lose track of time without realizing it, so setting timers with loud alarms or visual timers can be helpful to remind you of breaks.

You can use a timer to remind you how much time you have left or to check the actual time you are taking to perform a task. Timers can help you structure your tasks into short periods of focus time. You can use the Pomodoro method to work in chunks of 25 minutes. Other task manager apps like Sunsama have a built-in timer to track how much time a task took versus how much you had planned.

It's great to get motivated for a long time, don't get me wrong! But it is important to be aware of the total time you spend on something. A timer can be a great complement to remind you how much time you have left and decide how to use it intentionally.

Do Not Allow Others to Interrupt Your Flow Time

Feel free to block or set your calendar as "busy" for longer blocks of focused work or more meeting-free space. For example, some people work better alone in the morning and prefer meetings in the afternoon. Let them know or coordinate together what times are better to collaborate versus focus time.

Prioritize with purpose

Some coachees have shared that they find themselves surprisingly better at prioritizing when they're sick, extra busy, or even when they become new parents. Why is that? One reason could be that when we have more time, we use more than necessary. It is in line with Parkinson's Law.

Another reason could be that, in these moments, we prioritize tasks not because they are urgent (even though they are important and not yet due—"Do Later") but because they align with our passions or offer quick wins that provide a dopamine boost. In doing so, we may procrastinate on more urgent tasks.

Try to identify when you're doing this so that when you're in crisis mode, you can focus on what's truly urgent— even if you don't like it—and not get distracted by tasks that aren't immediately pressing. Write down those tasks on your backlog with a precise due date to work on them later.

Manipulating Your Environment to Support Your Flow

The Attention Deficit Disorder Association (ADDA)[xxvii] suggests making tedious tasks more interesting by having attractive and aesthetic office supplies, using fidget toys, or drawing, especially during exams or meetings.

I also support that idea, not only by creating an aesthetical workplace but also by keeping it organized and lean. In my book *5S Your Life*[xxviii], I emphasize the importance of an organized and clean environment to make it easier to focus and boost the pleasant flow state. The lean 5S methodology provides a framework to help you streamline your workspace and focus on what truly matters. You can create a productivity-friendly environment that supports your goals by applying these five principles—Sort, Store, Shine, Standardize, and Self-Organize.

The 5S Methodology

1. **Sort**: Begin by eliminating what's unnecessary from your workspace to focus on what is needed. Take time to remove items that don't contribute to your current work or long-term objectives. The goal is only to keep what you need at the moment. A clutter-free desk helps reduce mental clutter, allowing you to concentrate better on the tasks at hand.

2. **Store**: Once you've sorted your items, find designated places for everything you need. When each item has a specific spot or "home," you avoid the distractions of searching for things. A well-organized environment ensures that your tools are within reach when you need to focus, minimizing time wasted.

3. **Shine**: This step involves maintaining a clean and tidy workspace. Set a new level of cleanliness to maintain the needed items in good condition and be able to spot potential problems or delays quickly. Regularly cleaning your desk or work area helps to promote a clear mind. When everything is neat and orderly, you'll feel more prepared and motivated to tackle tasks without unnecessary distractions. This includes cleaning your desk or cleaning up software cookies.

4. **Standardize**: Create a system to sort, store and shine while you work without taking much of your time. Set rules for how your workspace should look and how tools should be arranged, ensuring that things don't get cluttered again over time. This step builds structure into your routine, making it easier to stay organized without having to think about it every day.

5. **Self-Organize**: Finally, repeat the 5S every day until they become a habit. Continually assess your environment and habits, adjusting them as needed. By regularly refining your workspace and workflow, you

create an environment that's always optimized for focus and productivity.

By following the **5S methodology**, you are creating a system that helps you keep your physical workspace organized and supports your mental clarity. Remember, you can use the 5s methodology for both physical and online organizations.

When you apply these principles consistently, your environment becomes a tool for your success, allowing you to focus better, reduce stress, and accomplish more in less time.

Start with something simple like organizing your desk and your laptop's desktop.

✦ PRO TIP: Commit to planning your day the night before. Identify and block out dedicated focus time, ideally during your peak energy hours. For example, set aside your morning power time (8 to 10 a.m.) for deep, challenging tasks that require maximum brainpower. Start with one-hour focus sessions, and gradually build your routine as you become more accurate in estimating task durations. Adjust your schedule as needed to avoid distractions and ensure you're making the most of your most productive time.

Emotional Shifts to Cultivate Flow with Compassion

Now, I would like to explore the more subtle aspects of achieving flow—not by changing behaviors but by managing your thoughts and feelings with compassion. Achieving flow isn't just about focusing on what you're doing; it's about how you approach the tasks at hand, the mental and emotional state you cultivate, and how you respond to the challenges along the way. By being mindful of your internal responses and turning routine activities into opportunities for engagement, you can access flow more easily and sustainably. This is where self-awareness and compassion for yourself play a critical role in navigating the complexities of daily life and work.

The Importance of Attention to Detail in Entering the State of Flow

Achieving flow requires keen attention to detail. When you're fully immersed in a task, the small elements—whether it's the precision of a written piece or the alignment of your thoughts—help guide you into that state of deep concentration. The more mindful you are of the nuances in your work, the easier it becomes to enter flow and maintain it. By focusing on the details, you engage in a rhythm that enhances your overall experience and makes the task feel less like work and more like an enjoyable challenge.

Why Purpose Matters?

According to scientists, the keys to longevity include a healthy diet, regular exercise, **finding a purpose in life** (an ikigai), and forming strong social connections. Members of the longest-living communities manage their time effectively to reduce stress, consume little meat or processed foods, drink alcohol in moderation, and stay physically active every day.

In the book *Ikigai: the Japanese Secret to a Long, Happy Life,* the authors highlight that "Existential frustration arises when our life is without purpose, or when that purpose is skewed."

In my view, just as every company needs a mission statement, every person needs a personal mission statement, purpose, Ikigai, or North Star to guide their decisions, emotions, and priorities—something that makes life worth living. When you know your North Star or who you want to be, all that's left to do is ensure that every day, you engage in activities that align with it and move you closer to that vision. For example, if my North Star is to become a coach who helps high performers and my own family reach their full potential, I am moving closer to my vision when I am coaching, writing, researching, and spending quality time with my kids. Each of these daily activities helps me enter a state of flow, making my day brighter, more purposeful, and effortless.

There are times when I feel demotivated or stressed as well, and I find myself wondering if there's something I should be doing more of—or something I should stop doing altogether, that doesn't align with my North Star.

While there might be challenges and setbacks, having a North Star helps you put things in perspective, prioritize and keep moving forward. Procrastination may creep in when you feel that activity is something that you're good at or you don't see how it tights to your own goals. Add purpose to that task or move it out of your backlog.

Challenge yourself with compassion to identify what truly matters to you and those you love. There may be times when you rush to accomplish tasks in a certain way, only to realize later that they aren't as important or urgent as you initially thought.

I asked one coachee what he had learned in our session after discussing flow and how to get motivated, and he said:

"Purpose may not be about becoming crazy motivated because I am doing that grandiose thing, like becoming a billionaire entrepreneur, but to be able to find that thing I love doing, where I can put my heart and soul every day."

✦ PRO TIP: If you're feeling unmotivated every day, take the time to discover your North Star and redefine the priorities of your daily tasks. Aligning your actions with what truly matters to you can reignite your sense of purpose and drive.

Turning Every Activity into Microflows

In his research, Csikszentmihalyi calls this transformation of routine tasks into moments of microflow a key to staying engaged. We've all experienced moments of boredom in class or at a conference, and to stay entertained, we start doodling or even whistling while painting a wall. When tasks aren't challenging enough, we add complexity to make them more engaging. This ability to turn ordinary activities into microflows—finding enjoyment and satisfaction in even the smallest tasks—is essential to happiness, say Hector Garcia and Francesc Miralles in their book *Ikigai*.

Everyone, no matter their success level, faces mundane tasks. Even Bill Gates washes the dishes every night. He says he enjoys it because it helps him relax and clear his mind. By focusing on improving the task each day—whether it's the way he stacks dishes or the order in which he cleans—he makes it a small challenge. This mindset of turning routine activities into microflows is a powerful tool for staying focused, relaxed, and in the moment.

Challenge Yourself

As I said before, one of the most powerful ways to stay engaged and maintain flow is by gradually making tasks a bit more challenging each time. Why not challenge yourself? When we push ourselves slightly beyond our comfort zone, our brains create new connections, which helps us stay energized and focused. This process of constant improvement fosters a sense of growth and keeps us motivated.

Whether by altering your routines, trying new approaches, or incorporating different habits into your day. Embracing small challenges can revitalize both your mind and your work, helping your experience flow more consistently.

I encourage my coachees to increase self-awareness about their routines, motivations and triggers for procrastination by using the Red and Green Exercise.

For one week, track your activities throughout your day and note how each makes you feel.

- **Yellow**: Are the tasks draining your energy or making you feel bored? Mark them as yellow.
- **Green**: Are you excited about them? Do they energize or bring you happiness? Mark them as green.
- **Red**: Do you feel angry, resentful, or even terrified when thinking about these tasks? Are you tempted to postpone, avoid, or get rid of them? Mark them as red.

This exercise helps you identify patterns in your procrastination, offering valuable insights into what fuels your resistance and what keeps you engaged and motivated. The more you focus on tasks that align with your passions and strengths, the more time you'll spend in a state of flow throughout your day. As a result, you'll notice that life feels smoother and more enjoyable as you're naturally drawn to what energizes and drives you.

Pushing Yourself with Compassion to Tackle Red Tasks

Sometimes, you procrastinate on certain tasks because they trigger negative emotions—anger, resentment, or even fear. These tasks can feel overwhelming or intimidating, making you tempted to avoid or postpone them. When this happens, mark these tasks as Red.

Red tasks are those that evoke strong emotional responses. You might dread them or feel a sense of resistance when thinking about them. By identifying them, you're not only acknowledging their emotional charge but also setting the stage to push through with compassion.

To approach these tasks, try reframing them with compassion. Recognize that your resistance is part of the process, and it's okay to feel this way. Instead of forcing yourself to tackle the task all at once, break it down into smaller, more manageable steps. Give yourself permission to approach the task gently, even if it's just for a few minutes. The key is to focus on the next small step rather than the overwhelming whole task.

If you're struggling to make progress, consider asking for help from a coworker, friend, or coach. They can help you analyze the cause of your frustration or negativity toward the task and offer fresh perspectives on how to approach it.

If you're facing many Red tasks throughout your day, it's worth considering how you can reduce them. Are there tasks that can be delegated or deferred? Or, can you transform these tasks into something more positive by reframing them as opportunities for growth or learning? By taking proactive steps to minimize or reframe your Red tasks, you can create space for more energy and focus on the things that align with your passions and strengths.

"Journaling was very helpful. It only took 10 minutes to reflect on what went well, like a good meal or a nice walk. It made me go to bed happy and satisfied and helped me sleep better."

Takeaways

- **State of Flow**: A mental state of deep immersion and focused energy in an activity, where time seems to disappear and the task feels effortless. It is often associated with high productivity and satisfaction.
- **Optimal Experience**: A state where individuals feel challenged but capable, experiencing high levels of engagement and intrinsic enjoyment. It's often linked to moments of peak performance and fulfillment.
- **Microflow**: The ability to turn routine or mundane tasks into moments of engagement by adding complexity or finding enjoyment, as described by Csikszentmihalyi.
- **North Star:** Your guiding purpose, often referred to as your *Ikigai*—the intersection of what you love, what you're good at, what the world needs, and what you can be rewarded for. Your North Star provides clarity and direction, helping you prioritize tasks and make decisions that align with your long-term vision and fulfillment.
- **Attention to Detail**: The focus on small elements of a task, which can help individuals enter and sustain the state of flow by deepening their engagement and concentration.
- **Compassionate Flow**: Managing your thoughts and feelings with kindness while engaging in tasks, allowing for more sustainable flow experiences without self-criticism.
- **Challenge-Skill Balance**: A key element of flow, where the challenge of the task is well-matched to the individual's skills, creating a sense of accomplishment and engagement.

Practical Tips to Cultivate Compassionate Flow TODAY

Write down Your North Star:

Take a moment to clearly define your *North Star*—your purpose, guiding principle, and core values. When you know what truly matters to you, it becomes easier to align your daily actions and decisions with that vision, bringing greater focus and meaning to your work. Write it down and revisit it regularly to stay grounded. The more your daily tasks align with your *North Star*, the more balance you'll achieve between productivity and well-being.

Choose One Task a Day That Drives You into Flow

Select at least one task each day that has the potential to engage you fully and bring you into a state of flow. This doesn't have to be a large or complex task—just one that excites you or challenges you in a way that feels motivating. Aim to focus for 15 minutes or an hour, but avoid setting unrealistic expectations like committing to four hours straight. Small, intentional blocks of time are often more effective at fostering flow than long, drawn-out sessions.

Challenge Yourself to Go the Extra Mile

Cultivating flow isn't just about setting timeframes; it's about pushing yourself slightly beyond your comfort zone in those things that you love doing so that you never get bored. Challenge yourself to take tasks a step further, adding just a bit more complexity or focus than you typically would. Improve that relationship that is not going very well, if you are playing tennis on level C, try to apply to level B or practice playing a new, more complex song. This will keep your brain engaged and help you progress, turning even routine tasks into opportunities for growth and deep concentration.

By adopting these simple practices, you'll work more effectively and enhance your wellbeing by finding enjoyment in the work itself. Compassionate flow is less about perfection and more about how you show up for yourself each day.

Download the worksheet for this chapter at www.lucypaulise.com/timebox

Chapter 7 | FINISH

Accept 'Finished for Now' and Move On with Purpose

How to complete your tasks with confidence, clarity and a sense of accomplishment.

"I have an A-type personality, so I've always strived for perfection. I want to excel at everything I do and push myself to achieve the highest standards."

Finishing is about more than just checking off tasks—it's about bringing them to a meaningful close with intention. Yet, in a world filled with distractions, endless comparisons, and competing priorities, completing what you start can feel like an uphill battle.

This chapter is about mastering the art of finishing. You'll learn how to overcome the perfectionism that keeps you stuck, eliminate barriers that prevent progress, and create a sense of accomplishment that fuels your motivation. By shifting your mindset from endless refinement to purposeful completion, you'll not only get more done but also approach your work with a more realistic and balanced perspective.

Jesse wants to progress in his career, feels stuck, but is too focused on growing, and is a perfectionist about the results, so he is also scared of change. All these feelings and overthinking are too overwhelming.

The Not Good Enough Effect

As you have seen, productivity isn't just about checking off every item on your to-do list; it's about prioritizing, recognizing what motivates you to do your best work, and, most importantly, defining what to finish and leave behind.

Now that you've learned how to stay focused and enter a flow state, the next step is determining when to call it a day without falling into the "Not Good Enough" (NGE) effect—the mental block that prevents you from declaring something finished. Easy to say, but not so easy to do, right?

One of the most frustrating aspects of time management is the feeling of ending the day with more tasks on your plate than when you started. This is especially true for multitaskers and procrastinators, but it's most pronounced in perfectionists and those struggling with imposter syndrome.

If you checked "perfectionist" on your time management test, you are most likely struggling with checking tasks off your list because you keep refining them, thinking, *What if this isn't good enough? What if someone finds a flaw? What if they realize I don't actually know what I'm doing?* These thoughts fuel an endless cycle of tweaking, reviewing, and second-guessing your work.

Even when you complete tasks, you might obsess over the outcome, question the quality, or assume that others will see it as inadequate. This prevents you from truly moving forward.

Imposter syndrome can be the hidden driver behind perfectionism, making you feel like you must overdeliver to prove your worth.

You might also find yourself stuck because:

- You don't ask for help, believing you *should* figure it out on your own.
- The task is too complex, and perfection feels unattainable.
- A manager or client keeps asking for revisions, reinforcing your fear that your work isn't good enough.

Ultimately, there will always be more details to refine, and the task remains a work in progress indefinitely. This is where self-compassion becomes essential—it allows you to recognize when "finished for now" is more valuable than chasing an impossible standard of perfection.

Getting to Done

In his book *The Age of Agile*, Stephen Denning[xxix] points out that one of the key reasons bureaucracies move slowly is the accumulation of partially finished tasks, each with unresolved problems. This "work in progress" can be wasteful, much like having half-finished products in a manufacturing process that take up space, use time and raw materials, and don't add value. The same principle applies to us in everyday life.

In agile methodologies, one of the most important practices is reducing work in progress by ensuring tasks "get done." It's not about starting tasks—it's about completing them to a clear and valuable standard. The key is to avoid accumulating partially completed tasks, which can cause bottlenecks and slow progress.

Therefore, to finish a task, it is necessary to have the following:

- A clear definition of done, meeting a specific set of criteria.
- Incremental progress, breaking tasks into small, manageable increments. Each part should be complete and ready for review before moving forward.
- Regularly review progress, adjusting strategies to eliminate mistakes early,
- Collaboration, regularly meeting with coworkers to provide status updates, communicate barriers and help each other.

The Power of Finishing

What does finishing a task mean in your daily life? It means making sure you check it off your list. Typical "almost finished" or NOT DONE tasks and activities are:

An email written in draft but not sent.

A code done but not tested.

A chapter written but not published.

A post stuck as a draft but not posted.

A presentation delivered but waiting for feedback.

The power of finishing lies in letting go of tasks to make progress. When it is not entirely finished, the task keeps holding a space in your brain, not just on your computer or in your office. That space prevents you from moving forward, distracts you, and can make you feel stressed and frustrated.

The psychological benefits of finishing tasks are profound and deeply rooted in our brain's reward system, making completing something highly satisfying and motivating. Here's how finishing tasks positively impacts us:

Boost in Dopamine Levels: Completing a task triggers the release of dopamine, a neurotransmitter associated with pleasure and reward. This "feel-good" chemical reinforces the behavior, making you more likely to pursue and complete future tasks. It creates a positive feedback loop where finishing leads to motivation to start and complete new tasks.

Reduction in Stress: We all remember unfinished tasks better than completed ones, called the *Zeigarnik effect*, where incomplete work consumes our mental energy. For example, you can't stop thinking about the laundry you didn't finish folding, that online offer you didn't take, or you're distracted by an unread text notification. Crossing tasks off your list provides closure, reduces mental clutter, and alleviates stress, offering relief and accomplishment.

Improved Mental Clarity: Along with reducing stress, finished tasks free up mental bandwidth, allowing you to focus on other priorities. This reduces overwhelm and enhances your ability to concentrate on the moment without being bogged down by undone work.

Sense of Satisfaction: A deep sense of fulfillment comes from bringing something to completion. This satisfaction is intrinsic—it doesn't rely on external validation but stems from seeing something through to the end. This can be particularly empowering for those prone to perfectionism.

Increased Self-Confidence: Finishing tasks builds confidence in your abilities. It sends a powerful message to your subconscious: "I can do this." Each completion reinforces a positive self-image and the belief that you're capable of handling challenges, which helps to combat self-doubt and perfectionism.

Momentum and Motivation: Success breeds success. Completing tasks creates a sense of momentum, making it easier to tackle subsequent ones. This is often called the "progress principle"—the more progress you make, the more motivated you feel to continue.

Building Resilience: Completing tasks, especially difficult or tedious ones, strengthens your resilience. It proves to yourself that you can overcome obstacles and follow through even when it's challenging. This builds grit and a sense of personal integrity.

Common reasons people struggle to finish tasks:

Once people overcome focus and flow, they may still struggle to finish tasks due to a variety of reasons, including:

- Lack of clarity or direction: When a task is unclear, or the steps are ambiguous, it can be challenging to know how to proceed.
- Lost in the details: Trying to perfect every detail can prevent people from moving forward, often stalling progress and making it difficult to consider a task "finished."
- Fear of success or change: Some individuals fear the responsibility of completing a task or the changes that will occur once it's finished, leading them to avoid finishing it subconsciously.
- Lack of accountability: Without external accountability, it's easier to leave tasks incomplete, especially if there's no urgency or consequence for not finishing.

- Burnout: If a person is overworked, they may lack the mental or physical capacity to follow through on tasks, especially if they're already stretched too thin.

By addressing these barriers, you can find strategies to improve task completion.

Question for you

What are your primary triggers for not being able to finish what you started?

Can you prioritize them so that you have your primary triggers at the top?

Common challenges from lack of finishing: Perfectionism and Giving Up

If you tend to be in **"fight" mode**, you likely react to challenges by pushing harder, working longer, and striving for unattainable perfection. Instead of strategizing or seeking assistance, you act impulsively, trying to overcompensate for fears—whether it's the fear of failure, criticism, or not being good enough. This often leads to obsessing over details, making it difficult to complete tasks. The irony? Perfectionism can also result in giving up entirely when the pressure becomes too overwhelming.

Challenge #1: Perfectionism

Perfectionism is often seen as a double-edged sword. On one hand, it fuels high-quality work and a drive for excellence. On the other, it creates unnecessary stress, anxiety, and frustration—sometimes even straining relationships. The obsession with flawless execution keeps you stuck, buried in minutiae, and unable to cross the finish line.

According to the Internal Family Systems (IFS) Theory[xxx], we all have different parts within us. One of these, the "firefighter," impulsively tries to protect us from failure and disappointment. For perfectionists, this part takes control by insisting that everything must be perfect before a task can be completed. As a result, you may work excessively, second-guess every decision, and revise endlessly—leading to burnout and an ongoing feeling of "never being done."

A coachee once shared:
"Hasta que no termine no me quedo tranquila."
"I can't feel at peace until I finish."

But the reality is this relentless pursuit of perfection means you rarely feel at peace at all. Instead of celebrating progress, you fixate on flaws, never allowing yourself to truly finish.

Perfectionism isn't just about working hard—it's about obsessing over quality and avoiding mistakes. For example, a perfectionist may spend hours tweaking the font size on a slide rather than focusing on the actual presentation content.

While attention to detail is valuable, perfectionism becomes problematic when it leads to unrealistic standards that are impossible to meet, a fear of making even minor mistakes, and a constant sense of dissatisfaction, even after delivering great work. Instead of moving forward, perfectionists often get stuck in an endless loop of refining and tweaking—never feeling like their work is truly done.

Beyond personal frustration, perfectionism doesn't just affect you—it impacts those around you as well. One of my coachees had a powerful realization about this:

"I always thought perfectionism was just self-inflicted pain, but I realized it affects others too. I make people upset when I spend too much time obsessing over details and miss deadlines—not just at work but with family and friends as well. I become short-tempered or preoccupied, and it strains my relationships. I finally understood that things don't always have to be perfect—sometimes, they just need to get done."

Perfectionism can lead to delays, frustration, and even resentment from colleagues, family, and friends who are impacted by your inability to let go of tasks. The key is recognizing when something is "good enough" and allowing yourself to move forward with confidence.

Instead of striving for impossible standards, shift your focus from perfection to progress. The key is knowing when something is truly done—not perfect, but purposefully complete. This allows you to learn from mistakes, move forward, and gain momentum without getting stuck in endless revision cycles.

Coping mechanism: When perfectionism takes over, you overcompensate by working excessively, believing that if you put in more effort, you can control the outcome and avoid failure or criticism. This provides temporary relief but leads to exhaustion, frustration, and diminished returns in the long run.

Challenge #2: The Fear of Finishing

While perfectionism can keep you stuck in an endless cycle of refinement, the opposite extreme is giving up entirely. When the fear of failure, change, or even success feels overwhelming, abandoning a task can seem like the safest option. Instead of overcompensating with excessive work, some people avoid finishing altogether—whether by procrastinating, delaying decisions, or walking away before completion.

This fear manifests in different ways. Some people start strong but abandon tasks halfway, worried they won't meet expectations when their imposter syndrome kicks in. Others postpone completion out of fear of being judged—thinking that as long as the task remains unfinished, no one can criticize the final result. The irony is that the longer you delay, the heavier the task feels, creating a cycle of avoidance and stress.

One of my coachees once admitted:

> *"I keep tweaking my work because I know people will have opinions about it once I finish. But the more I hold onto it, the more anxious I get. It feels safer to keep working on it forever than to let it go and face feedback."*

Breaking free from this cycle is key to shifting your mindset from perfection to progress. Instead of overworking or avoiding tasks, focus on setting realistic expectations: **not everything needs to be always flawless**; recognize the value of what's done, celebrate progress instead of only seeing what's left and committing to completion no matter what— define clear time limits to help you finish and move forward.

Coping mechanism: When fear of failure or criticism looms, giving up can be the safest way to avoid discomfort. The brain seeks relief by disengaging, convincing you that abandoning the task is better than facing potential imperfection or judgment. This avoidance strategy provides temporary ease but leads to long-term frustration, regret, and unfulfilled goals. That's why I like to remind myself of the song "Could Have Been Me" by Halsey.

Once you're in flow, the next step is learning when to stop refining and confidently call something "finished for now." By doing this, you get more done and develop the resilience and confidence needed to move forward, without fear holding you back.

✦ PRO TIP: **"Finished for now is better than never finished at all."**

Question for you

On a scale from 1 to 10, how would you rate your "get to finish" today?

(1 = Left many things unfinished, 10 = Completed with clarity, purpose and closure)

Behavioral Shifts To Get to Finish

Reflecting on how perfectionism impacts your life today can help you identify opportunities to transform it from a weight into a strength. Shifting your focus from the final outcome to the progress you're making—and practicing self-compassion along the way—can help you view life through a new lens. This mindset allows you to enjoy the present moment while continuing to move forward, even if the results don't meet your personal standards of "perfection."

It's all about finding balance in a world of extremes. As a perfectionist, you might naturally see things in black and white—something is either excellent or a failure. However, balance doesn't mean settling for mediocrity or ignoring important details. Instead, it's about navigating the middle ground. This involves understanding expectations, evaluating the costs and benefits of striving for perfection, and focusing your energy on the tasks that truly matter. By doing so, you can work on the right things for the right amount of time, avoiding overthinking and paving the way for meaningful progress.

Define the End of Your Day in Advance

Setting a specific time to finish your workday—and using an alarm or reminder to reinforce it—can help you resist the temptation to keep working endlessly. When working remotely or with a flexible schedule, it's easy to let your day blur into the evening as you try to check just one more thing off your list. Many employees struggle not only with taking breaks but also with defining a clear end to their workday. The result? It often feels like they never truly leave the "office," and personal and professional boundaries become increasingly blurred.

Do you ever feel like you must respond to every message or answer every call, no matter the time? Or tell yourself, "Just another 30 minutes to finish," only to find hours have passed, and neither the work nor your planned exercise happened? It's a common trap.

Surprisingly, psychological detachment—switching "off" from work at the end of your day—can lead to better engagement, creativity, and performance than simply working longer hours. Rest and recovery are essential, especially for perfectionists who demand high focus and detail in their work. Without proper rest, the quality of your efforts declines, no matter how long you stay at your desk.

By defining a precise end time for your workday, you're protecting your work-life balance and creating space to relax and recharge. This deliberate boundary ensures you're better prepared to tackle challenges the next day with renewed energy and focus.

Define A Healthy And Productive Shutdown Routine

To help you close your day, define a healthy shutdown routine. Add a 15-minute timebox to your calendar at the end of your day as a reminder of your shutdown routine if necessary. Some apps, like the Sunsama app, allow you to plan for a shutdown time right at the beginning of the day and show you a "Done for day" screen as a nudge to stop working and step away. Learn more about this app in the Recommended Tools section at the end of the book.

Use the last 15 minutes of your workday to review your accomplishments—identify at least one thing you're proud of completing. Then, update your to-do list for the next day, shut down your computer, and tidy up your workspace. This simple routine creates a clear boundary between work and personal time, helping you transition smoothly and mentally recharge for the next day.

Ending work on time gives you the space to make life more than just work and feel free and comfortable doing other things you enjoy, like having dinner with your spouse or doing your meditation routine, without checking the phone. Planning a shutdown time also helps you be realistic about how much time you have to accomplish your daily goals, hence being more positive at the end of the day about what you could accomplish.

Define the End of the Task in Advance

Just as setting a clear end time for your workday helps establish boundaries, defining what "done" means for a specific task prevents overworking and ensures you can finish confidently. Without clear criteria, it's easy to fall into the perfectionist trap of endless tweaks and second-guessing. Defining the finish line before starting saves time, energy, and mental strain.

To define what "done" means, consider these key components:

Set a "Finished For Now" Deadline

Determining how much time you will dedicate to a task is a powerful way to stay focused and prevent the task from expanding beyond what's necessary. For instance, you might decide, "I will work on this for one hour," or "I'll wrap this up by 3 p.m." Setting a time limit creates structure and reduces the tendency to overwork or get caught up in unnecessary details.

This approach is one of the most significant advantages of timeboxing. By allocating specific time blocks on your calendar, you manage your overall to-do list and control how much time you spend on each task. For example, if your workday runs from 8 a.m. to 6 p.m., you can schedule a realistic number of boxes to fit into that window. By visually limiting the time spent on a single task on your calendar, you shift your focus from perfection to progress, ensuring you get things done without falling into the trap of endless tweaking or overthinking.

"Finished for now" means giving a temporary closure that feels satisfying and accepting that it can be modified later. It's not an all-or-nothing situation.

Deliver or Share the Work

Clearly define the final step that marks the task as finished. For example:

○ **Sent:** If it's an email or report, sending it signals completion.

○ **Shared:** If it's a presentation or project, sharing it with the intended audience or a manager completes the task.

○ **Archived:** If it's a personal task, storing it in its final state (e.g., filing or saving) signifies closure.

For example, instead of saying, "I'll work on this report," redefine it as:

"Spend 90 minutes drafting the report."

"Log additional ideas in the parking lot."

"Email the draft to my manager by the end of the day."

The more specific you are, the better you know what to focus on to get the task done. This approach ensures you stay focused on the essentials while leaving room for improvement later if needed. You avoid wasting time on unnecessary tweaks for now, and you know exactly when the task is complete, so it helps in your self-talk to be compassionate about considering it done. It also encourages progress, freeing your mind to focus on other priorities.

Set Realistic Expectations for Quality

When planning a task, it's essential to set realistic expectations—not just for the time required but also for the quality of work you aim to achieve. Perfection isn't necessary for every task, and understanding what is truly expected can help you avoid overcommitting or overworking.

Consider factors like deadlines, priorities, and the level of detail required. While it's easy to fall into the trap of aiming for perfection, the additional time spent on perfecting every detail may not add meaningful value. By defining a clear and achievable quality standard, you can prevent burnout and focus on delivering the best possible results within the available time.

To better define realistic expectations, consider asking yourself and others the following questions:

1. **What kind of detail is expected?**
   Does the task require deep analysis and refinement, or will a high-level overview suffice?
2. **Who is going to review it?**
   Will the work be reviewed by a detail-oriented manager, a casual client, or a large team? Tailor your effort accordingly.
3. **What is a realistic deadline?**
   Does the deadline allow for a polished final product, or is speed the priority?
4. **What are the most critical aspects that cannot be overlooked?**
   Focus on the core elements that will have the most significant impact.

5. **Is it a draft or a final version?**
   If it's a draft, aim for completing on time over perfection. If it's the final version, prioritize essential details.

6. **What is at stake if you "mess up"?**
   Ask yourself: Can errors be corrected later, or is this a high-stakes, irreversible situation? Every task can feel like a life-changing moment for perfectionists—but is that truly the case here?
   Try setting a "perfection checkpoint." When you catch yourself over-editing or obsessing over small details, pause and ask: Would I notice this if someone else did it? If not, it's time to move on.

Set a Realistic Workload

Inadequate planning often sets the stage for failure. Common pitfalls include underestimating the time it takes to complete a project or spending too much time on initial tasks, leaving insufficient time for those at the end. A realistic workload isn't just about allocating the right duration for a single task—it's about considering all the other tasks that must be completed. This approach ensures that timeboxing remains practical and achievable.

When timeboxes are unrealistic, stress mounts as you scramble to finish on time. The goal isn't to leave tasks unfinished or to complete them poorly—especially if excellence is your hallmark. Unfortunately, dealing with unrealistic workloads is common, mainly when customers or project managers assign tasks without consulting the people responsible for execution. Lack of coordination and planning often leads to unfinished tasks or focusing on the wrong priorities.

If a project's timeline is set by someone else—like a project planner or client—evaluate whether the time allocated is sufficient before you start. If it's unrealistic, communicate your concerns upfront to set proper expectations. Consider asking:

- What needs to be done first?
- What is most important?
- Can the project be divided into milestones?
- What level of quality is realistically required?

✦ PRO TIP: If the timeline still seems unmanageable, propose alternatives:

- Focus on critical elements first and set a secondary deadline for the rest.
- Request deprioritization of other projects.
- Communicate the potential consequences of a reduced timeline, such as lower quality or missed deliverables.

Agreeing to an unrealistic timeline without discussion will only cause stress, reduce the quality of your work, and create more problems down the line.

Plan Daily for Realistic Success

While weekly planning can make everything seem achievable in theory, daily planning grounds your schedule in reality. For perfectionists, this approach is especially valuable—it allows you to factor in existing commitments, last-minute requests, and your actual energy levels when setting expectations. By planning day by day, you avoid overloading yourself and ensure your goals are realistic and attainable.

To build this habit, schedule a daily planning session—either at the end of the day to prepare for tomorrow or at the beginning of the day to set priorities. This small but powerful routine helps you stay flexible, focused, and in control of your time.

✦ PRO TIP: I plan my day before going to sleep.

Prioritize Before Rescheduling

Just as I mentioned in the *Focus* chapter about starting your day with the highest-priority tasks from your backlog, it's equally important to reassess as the day comes to a close. Before wrapping up, take a moment to determine what you can realistically finish and what needs to be moved to your *Do Later* list.

If certain tasks remain incomplete, prioritize what truly needs to be rescheduled versus what can wait. Avoid the temptation to overload yourself—pushing too hard can lead to burnout. Instead, commit to ending your workday at the scheduled time. If you happen to have extra time, revisit your backlog or use the opportunity for low-effort 2-minute tasks or admin tasks.

Break It Down

Again, use the concept of dividing larger tasks into smaller, manageable chunks that you can finish. For example, if you're writing a story, break it into steps like idea generation, drafting, formatting, and review. Set timeboxes of 25 minutes if you get distracted easily or 45 minutes for each task. If the timebox is not enough, add more timeboxes with smaller tasks. Always measure your task in terms of how many timeboxes you will use to finish it. By compartmentalizing, you allocate specific time for each part and avoid getting overwhelmed or losing focus. In my power time, for instance, I usually try to have two 45-minute timeboxes to finish my most complex tasks.

Underestimation Due To Excessive Refinement

Perfectionists often underestimate the time needed for tasks because they get caught up in continuous refinement and unnecessary details. You might spend hours tweaking aspects of your work that are already high quality, especially when there's no clear end in sight. If you have the luxury of time, allocate extra time for tasks that require your hyperfocus—just schedule it. For example, "I will spend two hours reviewing the format of my presentation." Timebox it. Before diving into work, challenge your thinking: not every detail deserves equal attention. Identify the most critical aspects of the task and timebox those first. Less important details can always be refined later if time allows.

Underestimating Time Due to Missing Details and Tasks

Poor planning often results from not accounting for all the steps needed to complete a task. For instance, you might estimate time for writing a report but forget to factor in time for research, formatting, proofreading, or approvals. Similarly, neglecting smaller but essential tasks—such as responding to emails, preparing for meetings, or handling administrative work—can lead to unexpected time shortages. To avoid this, use a timebox for every single task. Plan thoroughly to ensure a balanced workload and avoid last-minute rushes. If you realize you don't have enough time to complete everything, use the

4Ds: Can you delegate some tasks, defer them, or delete them? Or, can you adjust the quality to meet the time constraints?

Timebox for Double the Time

Despite your best planning, surprises happen. Besides adding buffers as suggested in the Timeboxing chapter, identify if there are some tasks that you tend to underestimate or spend more time on, usually creative or complex tasks. Timebox for double the time, to be more exact.

For example, if you can finish something in one hour, estimate at least 1.5 or 2 hours and schedule it on your calendar to better plan your day.

This buffer accounts for the unexpected—whether it's last-minute revisions, unforeseen challenges, or simply the time it takes to refine the quality of your work. By giving yourself this extra time, you avoid the pressure of rushing and can maintain a balanced approach to task completion. This also allows for flexibility in case you need to adjust your expectations for quality as you progress through the task. Naturally, this approach will be more realistic, but it will also force you to prioritize what tasks need to be done first, which ones *really* require double time, and which ones can be taken more lightly.

The "Do Later" Parking Lot: Additional Details

If you find new ideas or details you want to explore further, jot them down in a "Do Later parking lot" list. These are incredibly valuable and often what set you apart and contribute to your success! But these could take up to 25% of your time, delaying your final result or making it "impossible to finish." This lets you save those ideas for later without derailing your progress. If time permits, you can revisit them, but if not, the task can still be considered complete.

This can be a document, a post-it note, or a backlog where you collect and store ideas for future use. It's your depository for those "nice-to-have" tasks and ideas that you can revisit whenever you have more time or a specific need arises.

The "Love All" Parking Lot: When to Step Back

In The Inner Game of Tennis, Timothy Gallwey explains, "The secret of winning any game lies in trying not too hard." Trying too hard can paralyze progress instead of improving performance. The same applies to time management. When you're stuck, overthinking, or endlessly refining a task, the best strategy might not be to push harder—it might be to drop the racket.

It's a cue to recognize when effort has become counterproductive. If you're stuck on a task, rewriting the same email for the tenth time, or obsessing over tiny details that don't add value, it's time to step back, reset, and refocus. This doesn't mean giving up—it means:

- Pausing to regain clarity before diving back in.
- Asking for help or feedback instead of struggling alone.
- Shifting to a different task to return later with a fresh mind.

In Tennis, "Love" Means Zero

But in life, that can be a beautiful reminder. Even when you've made mistakes, missed the mark, or feel like you're starting from nothing—you're still in the game. And you still deserve love.

Self-compassion means giving yourself grace when the scoreboard shows zero and trying again with curiosity, not judgment. Because just like in tennis, every point is a chance to reset. Move your task to the "Love all" parking lot when you're stuck in analysis paralysis, you've been refining something endlessly without real improvement, you're forcing productivity but feel mentally drained, or a task that should take 30 minutes has now taken 3 hours.

Mark it to check later with a fresh mindset during your next Power Time the following day, or consult someone else—ask a coach, mentor, or colleague for quick feedback before giving up or skipping your family dinner.

How do you know when it is time to drop the racket and love all? This is how a coachee expressed it from her perspective:

> " I pause when I sense that gut feeling, a knot close to my stomach telling me, 'it's enough, I have done enough'. It's time to pause and not blame myself."

✦ PRO TIP: Just like in tennis, your shots suffer if you grip the racket too tightly. Loosening your grip—mentally and physically—allows you to perform with more ease, flow, and confidence. So next time you're stuck, drop the racket, love yourself and park it for later, and return when you're ready to make real progress.

Manage Up Your Micro-manager

Perfectionism, procrastination and poor planning can sometimes stem from management issues, mainly when managers are overly critical, excessively focused on details, or prone to micromanaging. When leaders with perfectionist tendencies are excessively harsh in their feedback, their employees may become fearful of making mistakes. This can lead employees to avoid sending an email because they feel it isn't good enough or spend too much time in the review process to make it "perfect."

Micro-managers often develop unproductive habits that hinder progress, such as:

- Treating everything as urgent.
- Underestimating the time required to complete tasks.
- Adding unnecessary steps or reviews, resulting in incomplete projects.

Additionally, micromanagers may force employees to switch between tasks based on shifting priorities, leaving critical work unfinished. While some re-prioritization is necessary, it's essential to have clear discussions about deadlines and task management to avoid inefficiency. Overcontrolling in the name of perfectionism is stressful, time-consuming, and ultimately counterproductive.

Managing up means creating a mutually beneficial relationship with your manager to improve communication, collaboration, and efficiency while maintaining your boundaries. Whether you constantly adapt to your boss's preferences or resist managing up altogether, there's a balanced middle ground.

In fact, Gallup research shows that 70% of the variance in team engagement is attributable to the manager[xxxi]. Striking the right balance between impressing your higher-ups and maintaining your work-life equilibrium is key to sustained success. Here's how to manage up without sacrificing your wellbeing:

Prioritize communication

Keep your manager updated on your progress, challenges, and contributions. Understanding their preferred communication style (e.g., brief vs. detailed, calls vs. emails) helps reduce misunderstandings. Regular updates also build trust and minimize last-minute requests that could lead to overworking.

Understand their priorities

Take time to learn your manager's goals, objectives, and preferences. By aligning your efforts with what matters most to them, you can focus on high-impact tasks and reduce the pressure of unnecessary overtime.

Set Clear Boundaries

Define and communicate your work hours and stick to them. Timeboxing can help manage expectations and reassure micromanagers of your professionalism and autonomy. Share your schedule or task list to show you're staying on track while protecting your personal time. Set clear boundaries regarding what is acceptable for you and what is not. This can include work start time, finish time, lunchtime, focus time in the morning or afternoon or preferences about how you want others to reach out to you, to name a few. Be very specific about what you need. Ending on time, beginning early, or respecting personal time may not mean the same to others.

Showcase results, not hours

Shift the narrative from how much time you spend working to what you achieve. Highlight your contributions during meetings and reports to ensure your value is recognized without needing to overextend yourself.

Highlight your wins

If your manager isn't naturally inclined to recognize accomplishments, take the initiative. Share your achievements and emphasize their impact. This is especially important if your boss is new to their role or unfamiliar with the specifics of your work.

Cover for your boss

Whenever possible, and the job is within your wheelhouse, help to support their weaknesses. Instead of complaining about your manager's shortcomings, find ways to support them. If they're consistently late to meetings, offer to kick things off. If they're slow to respond, use the downtime to make further progress on projects. This proactive approach fosters goodwill and teamwork.

Effectively managing up requires intentionality and balance, but it pays off in the long run. Building a positive, collaborative relationship with your manager benefits not only you but also your team and organization. By focusing on communication, prioritization, and boundaries, you can thrive under any leadership style while maintaining your wellbeing.

Communicate your needs

Communicating boundaries is not only for your boss but also for your coworkers, family and friends. You can have a specific conversation or agreement with your closest colleagues if you turn off the notifications or use the "Do Not Disturb" mode at a particular time or when doing a specific job. If you work on a team that shares daily updates, you can post to Slack at the end of the day what you accomplished as a tremendous async alternative to standup meetings and also let them know that you will be off until the next day.

✦ PRO TIP: it will be challenging to keep these boundaries, especially when working with people in other time zones or with colleges that have not set their own boundaries yet. Take your time and breath. Trust that this change is part of your decision to care for yourself and prevent burnout.

Seek feedback

Schedule regular check-ins with a coach, a manager or an accountability partner to discuss your progress and make adjustments as needed. This will help you stay accountable and focused on your long-term objectives.

Share your work with your team if you are stuck or keep finding areas to improve. Another pair of eyes may help you decide when it's acceptable to finish. Double-check with your teammates what the expectations are and what a realistic deadline looks like in every project or commitment.

Emotional Shifts to Cultivate Finishing with Compassion

Even small tasks can feel monumental for perfectionists, leading to unnecessary stress and a fear of failure. Repurpose emotions like self-doubt, shame, fear, and guilt—they may be painful, but they are simply trying to protect you. When you tell yourself that no matter how much effort you put in, success feels out of reach, it could be a part of you attempting to shield you.

This part might stem from past experiences where someone micromanaged you or was overly critical of your success, and now it's working to prevent you from feeling that same pain again. Recognizing this protective impulse allows you to respond with compassion and shift your focus to finishing with a sense of achievement, not perfection.

To counter this, take time to assess the real stakes. Ask yourself:

- **What is the worst-case scenario?** Is it truly catastrophic, or is it manageable?
- **How can I mitigate risks?** Are there steps you can take to reduce the likelihood of errors or adjust your approach if something goes wrong?
- **How can I prioritize?** If unexpected challenges arise, what is the minimum you can deliver to meet expectations without sacrificing quality?

These questions aren't just about clarifying expectations with managers or clients—they're also about putting tasks into perspective so you can confidently approach them and sleep peacefully at night.

If you don't take the time to ask these questions, you risk setting yourself up for unspoken, unrealistic expectations. Managers or clients may begin expecting a gold-medal effort every time, which can create unsustainable workloads. While striving for excellence is commendable, not every task requires the same effort.

Accept "finished for now," a New Definition of Done

"The load continues—it feels like there's never a real sense of completion to anything."

Perfection is often unattainable, and expecting to finish everything on your plate by the end of the day is just as unrealistic. The truth is that the workload will always continue—but that doesn't mean you're falling behind. Shifting your perspective from "I must finish everything" to "I am finishing what matters most for now" can be incredibly freeing.

To get something done, it doesn't necessarily need to be perfect. Understand that "finished for now" is a balance between perfect and sustainable, especially when deadlines are tight.

People say perfection is the enemy of action, but I think it is more accurate to say that perfection is the enemy of closure. Starting is not as difficult as closing when you are focused on the details. To close a task or a project, you need to be able to dedicate a certain amount of time to the endeavor and accept what you have done, which can be the most difficult part.

A task that can be done in an hour or 10 hours if you strive for perfection, thanks again to Parkinson's law.

The main questions to ask yourself are:

Is it worth it?

How many other tasks are you doing instead?

Is quality more important than quantity for this particular job?

If attention to detail and excellent quality are expected, you need to consider them in the timeline. Suppose you can use 10 hours, not only one hour, to create that design; plan for 10 hours. But still, it doesn't mean there will be enough time to make it perfect. Remember Parkinson's law: if you have 10 hours, you will use them. That is why sometimes you wonder why many people quit working and still feel overwhelmed.

If you only have one hour to make the design, prioritize what needs to be done first, and leave the details to the end or keep them on your Defer Parking lot.

✦ PRO TIP: Most times, our work is not good enough for us, but it is good enough for the rest of the world, so go ahead and put it forward!

Respect your time box in your calendar, and don't spend more time on each task than needed! Accept what you accomplished.

The Recipe to Shine: Progress And Consistency

Thoughts like "This is so hard, I can't do this," or "This is so boring, I hate it" are common. Cognitive Behavioral Therapy (CBT)[xxxii] for perfectionism recommends shifting your focus from the negative. Instead of getting stuck in self-critical thoughts, try re-framing them to acknowledge the positives: "This is a challenge, but I actually like learning new things."

In *Mindset* by Carol Dweck[xxxiii], the concept of a growth mindset is emphasized as the belief that abilities and intelligence can be developed through dedication, effort, and learning. Instead of seeing mistakes as failures, a growth mindset encourages you to view them as opportunities for growth.

When you make a mistake, focus on the lessons learned and celebrate the process of learning and improving. That is to make progress. This mindset shifts the perspective from a fixed view—where mistakes are seen as setbacks or signs of failure—to an empowering view that mistakes are integral to your development and ultimate success. Adopting a growth mindset that values progress over perfection helps foster resilience, adaptability, and an ongoing commitment to learning.

As someone who loves sports, I've learned that activities like running, skating, or playing tennis become more valuable through consistent repetition rather than striving for perfection. What will make you shine in the long term is not one perfect routine but maintaining the routine over time, even when conditions aren't ideal—whether you're short on time or not feeling your best. My best tennis days were super cold, but I still attended the class. Consistency trumps perfection. Committing to showing up regularly, even on imperfect days, builds momentum, strengthens positive habits, and unlocks long-term benefits that far outweigh the temporary desire for flawless execution. Embracing this mindset in sports can be applied to many other areas of life, helping you move forward despite obstacles.

Shift From "Perfect" To "Purposeful"

Ask yourself: Does this serve its **purpose** (is it functional, valuable, and ready to use, or does it align with your North Star)? If the answer is yes, move on. If the answer is no, identify the smallest purposeful improvement or step you can take and make it—then move on.

You can also shift your focus from the desired outcome to the purpose of the task and the steps needed to complete it. For example, if you're tasked with calling clients, your primary goal may be to meet a quota or become the top salesperson of the month. Instead of obsessing over the specific outcome of each call, concentrate on engaging with each client and taking the necessary steps to guide them toward saying "yes." Remember, the final result is not entirely in your control, but the process is.

Measuring success by progress, consistency and purpose rather than flawlessness makes you more likely to stay motivated and push through the task. Emphasize the small wins and steps along the way, and you'll find yourself motivated to keep moving forward, no matter what.

"He who has a why to live for can bear almost any how."

Friedrich Nietzsche, Twilight of the Idols.

Accept Closure and Let Go

Overcoming the fear of finishing begins by embracing closure as an integral part of your growth process. Instead of viewing completion as the end of your work, see it as a natural step in its evolution. Understand that not every task will be flawless, and sometimes, you need to let go to keep moving forward.

In the tech industry, the concept of "technical debt" refers to accepting a certain level of work quality, acknowledging that more could be done but choosing to postpone it to complete the task at hand. By accepting the work as it is, you allow yourself to progress, with the understanding that if time permits, you can revisit and improve it later.

I often remind my clients that finishing an email or closing a project isn't necessarily a "never again" moment—it's more likely a "good for now." Think of it as a step or a Minimum Viable Product (MVP), as Lean Startup methodology suggests. It's something that can always be iterated upon, revamped, or enhanced at a later time. Embrace "good for now" as a stage, not a final act.

Additionally, release any task or project you cannot complete at the moment. Holding onto unfinished work can drain your energy and prevent you from progressing. Letting go creates space for new opportunities, learning experiences, and the freedom to focus on what truly matters.

Understanding Imposter Syndrome

As you work toward mastering the art of finishing, one of the biggest emotional barriers that may hold you back is imposter syndrome—the persistent belief that you are not as competent as others perceive you to be. Even with evidence of success, you may still feel like a fraud, fearing that at any moment, someone will "find out" that you don't actually belong.

Clance and Gail Matthews[xxxiv] found that nearly 70% of people experience imposter syndrome at some point in their careers. This is especially prevalent in remote work environments, where employees may receive less real-time feedback from managers and have fewer opportunities for visibility, making it harder to validate their own performance.

Imposter syndrome is a cognitive distortion that prevents you from fully internalizing your accomplishments. You may rationalize your success as luck, timing, or the result of external factors rather than your own abilities. This can lead to self-sabotaging behaviors such as overworking, seeking constant external validation, procrastinating out of fear, or struggling with perfectionism.

Some of the key signs of imposter syndrome include:

- Overworking to compensate for perceived inadequacy leads to burnout.
- Downplaying your skills and accumulating unnecessary certifications to "prove" your worth.
- Perfectionism, where nothing ever feels good enough, and you revise endlessly.
- Seeking constant validation from mentors or peers to confirm that you are doing well.
- Comparing yourself to others, always questioning why someone else received a promotion, higher salary, or recognition.
- Struggling with confidence, hesitating to speak up or contribute ideas in fear of being exposed as "not knowledgeable enough."
- Viewing success in extremes—you are either the best or the worst, with no in-between.
- People-pleasing, prioritizing others' expectations over your own needs to feel valued.

If you resonate with any of the above, you might notice how imposter syndrome affects your ability to finish your work. You may keep refining projects, pushing deadlines, or avoiding completing tasks because finishing means exposing your work to others—making you feel vulnerable to criticism or failure.

This creates a cycle: You work excessively, struggle to let go of tasks, and still don't feel like it's enough. The pressure to constantly prove yourself means you never feel fully satisfied with your accomplishments, no matter how much you achieve.

To overcome the imposter syndrome trap, compassion becomes essential. Instead of seeing finishing as a test of worthiness, shift your mindset to purposeful completion— acknowledging that your work is enough for now. Accepting your strengths, celebrating progress, and letting go of unattainable perfection will help you finish with confidence rather than fear.

The ABCD of Positive Self-Talk

How do you say no or let go when your inner critic won't stop talking? That harsh self-talk in your head might sound like: *"Why didn't I try harder? What's wrong with me?"* When things don't go as planned, negative self-talk often takes over, triggering anxiety and placing your nervous system in threat mode. Your body prepares to respond—fight, flight, or freeze—but you get stuck overthinking instead of acting.

This internal spiral doesn't just drain your confidence— it hijacks your productivity. You waste time ruminating, second-guessing decisions, and revisiting tasks instead of completing them. Even simple priorities feel overwhelming when your brain is flooded with fear and self-judgment.

To break that cycle, your mind needs a reset—from fear to clarity, judgment to compassion, spinning to acting.

That's where **The ABCD of Self-Talk** comes in. This simple yet powerful method helps you move from self-criticism and mental chaos to taking a practical step. It blends awareness, breathwork, compassion, and forward movement so you can forgive yourself, reframe negative thoughts, and take meaningful action—even when things don't go as planned.

Here are the four steps:

1. Awareness

The first step in transforming your self-talk is awareness. Recognize the negative or unhelpful thoughts that arise. Notice when you are being overly critical or harsh with yourself. These self-sabotaging thoughts often run on autopilot, but once you catch them, you can begin to create the space for choice—and change.

2. Breath

Take a deep breath. This simple step helps interrupt the cycle of negative self-talk and gives you space to respond thoughtfully rather than impulsively. Deep breathing helps activate the parasympathetic nervous system, calming your mind and body, which can create more clarity and emotional control in moments of self-doubt or stress. It tells your brain, *"You're safe. You don't need to run. Let's slow down."* This pause gives you enough space to move from reactive to intentional thinking.

3. Challenge With Compassion

Now that your mind is calmer, you can challenge your negative thoughts with compassion. Ask yourself:

* Is this thought based on facts or assumptions?

What would I say to a friend who was thinking this about themselves?

We often hold ourselves to impossible standards—expecting perfection, immediate results, or constant strength. But you deserve the same kindness and empathy you would offer someone else.

Reframe your thinking not with toxic positivity, but with grounded compassion. You can tell yourself, "It's understandable that I feel this way right now." Let that validation create space for perspective. An then, zoom out. Visualize your big picture and long-term goals. Are you still on track overall? How far have you already come? Remind yourself of past wins, strengths, and resilience. Progress isn't always linear, but you're moving forward—even if it doesn't feel like it in the moment.

4.   Do Something About It

At its core, negative self-talk is often your brain's way of trying to protect you—it's sounding the alarm to help you prepare, defend, or respond. But when no action follows, your mind keeps spinning, searching for resolution. That's why the spiral won't stop until you give it direction.

Once you've reframed your thoughts with compassion, the next step is to **take action**. Define one small, practical step you can take—something achievable and clear. Break the task down if needed. Even the smallest action helps shift your brain from a state of overwhelm into a sense of agency.

Progress quiets the inner critic. A clear action plan allows you to regain control, stop the spiral, and move forward with intention.

End Your Day with Positivity: The Losada Ratio in Action

What happens when you don't have time to reflect on your shutdown routine—when you're rushing from work to pick up your kids, cook dinner, or finally play that game you've been waiting for? Even on the busiest of days, taking just five minutes before bed to reflect can make a huge difference.

Studies on the Losada Ratio[xxxv] suggest that for every negative thought or experience, focusing on three positive ones helps break the cycle of stress and negativity. This simple yet powerful practice shifts your mindset, promoting greater resilience, relaxation, and better sleep.

✦ PRO TIP: Tonight, before you go to bed, take a moment to identify **three things you're proud of accomplishing today**—big or small. By training your brain to recognize and celebrate progress, you cultivate happiness, self-compassion, and a sense of fulfillment, even on the most chaotic days.

Celebrate Progress Intentionally

At the end of your day, take time to review your progress. Identify which tasks were completed, which ones need to be carried over to the next day, and where you may need support. Celebrating your accomplishments is essential— reward yourself for completing tasks and acknowledge your efforts.

When you finish a task, reflect on what went wrong, probably your default mode, and **what went right**. Apply the 3-to-1 principle (or the Losada ratio), thinking of three positive aspects or thoughts for each improvement or negative thought.

This balanced reflection fosters a mindset of growth and encouragement.

By reviewing your progress and internalizing your wins, you train your mind to embrace positive self-talk instead of self-criticism.

Instead of judging unfinished tasks, celebrate what you did accomplish. Being able to focus on a challenging or tedious task deserves recognition. Treat yourself—a nice snack, a walk outside, or a relaxing activity—when you complete something significant. Rewards reinforce positive habits and make focusing more enjoyable.

Celebrate Partial Successes, Too

As a perfectionist, it's easy to think in extremes: either something is perfect, or it's a failure. This all-or-nothing mindset can prevent progress, especially when setting high expectations for yourself. For example, if your goal is to exercise for 60 minutes a day, you may skip it entirely if you don't have a full hour to dedicate. Instead, focus on celebrating partial successes. Even committing to just 15 minutes of exercise is a win. This shift in mindset helps rewire your thinking and reduces the pressure to be perfect. It's not a failure to complete a 15-minute workout instead of a full 60-minute run—it's progress.

Rather than setting rigid goals like "exercise 60 minutes every day at 9 am," try setting a more achievable goal, like "exercise every day." This approach allows for flexibility and emphasizes consistent effort over perfection. Recognize and reward yourself for completing tasks, even if they are small milestones toward a larger goal. This reinforces positive behaviors, reduces the fear of starting new tasks, and helps build self-compassion by acknowledging that progress, not perfection, is what matters.

Get a Coach

A coach, accountability partner, or manager can play a crucial role in helping you shift your emotional intelligence and overcome the perfectionism that can often hold you back from finishing tasks. An external source of support can help break this cycle by offering constructive feedback and encouragement, fostering a compassionate approach to task completion.

A coach can help you understand and manage the underlying emotional drivers behind perfectionism and explore the fears or beliefs that cause you to stall or overanalyze when your boss cannot do it for you. They work with you to build self-compassion and emotional resilience, teaching you how to make decisions and take action without being paralyzed by the need to get everything perfect. Through coaching, you can develop the self-awareness to recognize when perfectionism is hindering your progress, and you can practice shifting your emotional response to tasks, focusing on completion and growth instead of flawlessness.

An accountability partner or a buddy could be a coworker, friend or family member who can provide regular check-ins, ensuring that you stay focused on progress rather than perfection. You can also have regular check-ins with your managers to help alleviate perfectionism by setting clear expectations and fostering a supportive environment.

Takeaways

- **"Not Good Enough" (NGE) Effect:** A mental barrier that prevents us from declaring a task finished due to fear of imperfection, leading to procrastination or unfinished work.
- **Work in Progress:** Tasks that remain unfinished accumulate in your pipeline, causing bottlenecks and slowing progress, often leading to feelings of overwhelm.
- **Imposter Syndrome:** the persistent and paralyzing belief that you are not as competent as others perceive you to be.
- **Dopamine:** A neurotransmitter released when completing a task or making progress, triggering feelings of pleasure and rewarding achievement.
- **Shutdown Routine:** A structured process for wrapping up work at the end of the day, helping to disconnect and reset for the next session.
- **Perfectionism:** The constant pursuit of flawlessness, which can hinder progress by focusing too much on minute details or unrealistic expectations.
- **Saying No:** The act of setting boundaries by declining requests or tasks that don't align with your priorities or capacity.
- **Realistic Expectations:** Setting achievable, well-defined goals and standards that account for current capabilities, time, and resources.
- **Do Later Parking Lot:** A strategy for temporarily postponing tasks or ideas that are not immediately important or relevant, ensuring they don't distract from current priorities.
- **Love All parking lot:** A strategy to postpone tasks intentionally when you're stuck in analysis paralysis, or you've been refining something endlessly without real improvement.

- **Managing Up:** Effectively communicating with and supporting your supervisor or manager, ensuring alignment and clear expectations.
- **Setting Boundaries:** Defining limits on your time, energy, and resources to maintain focus and wellbeing while protecting yourself from overwhelm.
- **Finished for Now:** Accepting that something doesn't have to be perfect to be functional; a way of moving forward by doing what's needed at the moment.
- **The ABCD of Positive Self-Talk:** A framework for shifting negative self-talk to positive, starting with **A**wareness, **B**reath, **C**hallenging your thoughts with **C**ompassion and **D**oing something about it.

Practical Tips to Cultivate Finishing Tasks with Compassion

End-of-Day Reflection: At the end of your day, practice the Losada ratio by thinking of 3 things you are proud you accomplished that day. If you start judging yourself instead for unfinished tasks, kindly remind yourself also to recognize and celebrate what went well.

Daily check-in: Practice the ABCD of Positive Self-Talk every time you feel you are getting anxious or stressed by a task that needs completion.

Download the worksheet for this chapter at www.lucypaulise.com/timebox

Chapter 8 | COMPASSION

Review your progress with a balanced and realistic self-care approach.

How to maintain a healthy balance between productivity and wellbeing.

Me - "What goes through your mind when you hear all these great reviews from your coworkers?"

Coachee - "It feels completely opposite to how I see myself. They recognize everything I'm accomplishing, but behind the curtains, I feel like I haven't done enough."

If you've ever felt this way, you're not alone. Many high-achievers experience this disconnect—externally praised for their success while internally battling feelings of inadequacy. This tension between passion and self-doubt is more common than you think.

Healthy Passion: Why Compassion Matters

Passion and self-compassion are deeply intertwined, especially when it comes to sustaining long-term success and personal fulfillment.

Passion is a powerful motivator, pushing individuals to pursue ambitious goals with enthusiasm and determination. However, when passion isn't balanced with self-compassion, it can lead to burnout, stress, and feelings of never doing enough—just like my coachee described.

I hear the word "overwhelmed" frequently from high-achievers. They set high expectations for themselves yet struggle to recognize their progress. This is where self-compassion becomes essential—not as an excuse to lower standards but as a tool to sustain passion in a way that fuels rather than depletes.

What Is Self-Compassion

Kristin Neff[xxxvi], a leading researcher on self-compassion, says that:

Self-appreciation and self-compassion are really two sides of the same coin. One is focused on what brings us pleasure, the other on what brings us suffering. One celebrates our strengths as humans; the other accepts our weaknesses.

What really matters is that our hearts and
minds are open. Rather than continually
evaluating, comparing, resisting, obsessing,
and distorting—we simply open. Open to
seeing ourselves and our lives exactly as
they are, in all their glory and ignominy.
Open to the love of all creation, ourselves
included, without exception.

We don't need to be perfect to feel good about ourselves, and our lives don't need to be any certain way for us to be content.

Rather than multitasking, overworking, driving yourself to perfection or becoming overwhelmed by external expectations, self-compassion helps you recognize your limits and acknowledge that taking breaks, adjusting goals, or seeking help is okay.

Self-compassion allows you to nurture your passion without self-judgment, leading to sustainable growth and creativity. It helps individuals recognize that failure or struggle is part of the journey, not a reflection of their worth. This keeps their passion alive without draining their mental or emotional energy.

In essence, self-compassion ensures that your passion remains a source of joy and purpose rather than becoming a source of stress or dissatisfaction. When you practice self-compassion, you are more likely to persist with your passion in a healthy, fulfilling way.

Dealing with your inner critic can be challenging in a competitive and demanding work environment. Self-compassion can help you develop healthier coping behaviors.

Our brain has complex functions that differ from other species, enabling us to imagine and plan for the future, ruminate, and worry. While you utilize these functions, you may get caught up in negative self-talk loops that distract and drive anxiety or depression, which are not helpful, such as "I will mess up on this presentation" or "They will think I am not knowledgeable enough." You become your worst enemy.

Self-compassion, instead, is a way to support yourself through your struggles. But what exactly is self-compassion? It's the ability to treat yourself with kindness, especially when facing setbacks. It's responding to your inner critic with "It's OK, let's keep trying"—or even better, "Let's keep trying, but without forcing it."

Think of it like tennis: The best players don't improve by *trying harder*; they improve by *allowing themselves to play*—trusting their instincts, making adjustments, and letting the game flow. But here's the key: they still train every day. They practice the drills, refine their technique, and build muscle memory so that when it's time to play, their body knows what to do. They focus on the process, not just the result.

The same applies to your goals. You don't have to push yourself to exhaustion, but you do need to show up, train, and trust that your preparation will carry you forward. In the long run, you're still in charge—you set the pace, and with consistent effort, you can win. Progress isn't about perfection; it's about refining your approach, staying committed, and giving your best—without the weight of unrealistic expectations.

One of the key components of self-compassion is recognizing your shared humanity and embracing the reality that nobody is perfect. View a setback or a mistake as a learning opportunity and respond to yourself with empathy. You can help your mind get out of the loop, focus on a positive outlook and regain self-confidence.

A recent study led by Madeleine Ferrari[xxxvii] found that self-compassion can help protect against depression in people with perfectionistic tendencies. The study showed that self-compassion "consistently reduces the strength of the relationship between maladaptive perfectionism and depression for both adolescents and adults."

In their book, The Compassionate Mind Workbook, Chris Iron and Elaine Beaumont[xxxviii] explain that by recognizing that "your brain can be tricky" and understanding that it is normal to get caught in negative thoughts that you don't always need to pay attention to, you can learn to create a different loop and stop blaming yourself.

The Reverse Flow

I call this loop of negative thoughts the reverse flow. An unexpected email, a colleague drops the ball, or a high-stakes presentation goes sideways, and suddenly, the pressure builds your confidence drops, and mistakes compound. You're not just distracted—you're stuck in the reverse flow.

It's like being in a mental tailspin, a state of flow but destructive. And the more you try to regain control, the worse it gets. Sound familiar? High performers often experience reverse flow not because they lack skill—but because they care deeply. The key isn't pushing harder. It's learning how to pause, reset, and take back control of your attention.

When pressure rises, your ability to reset your focus to get out of the reverse flow is what separates a rough patch from a full-blown derailment.

The good news is that self-compassion is not a genetic trait; you can be taught to be kind to yourself.

Shine Through Your Strengths

"I compare myself to others,
idealizing their strengths while minimizing
my own."

When you constantly compare yourself to others, you reinforce self-criticism rather than self-compassion. You see others' achievements through a magnifying glass while downplaying your own. But true self-compassion involves recognizing and appreciating your unique strengths—not just dwelling on what you lack.

The first step in building self-confidence is acknowledging and embracing your strengths. Instead of focusing on perceived shortcomings, shift your perspective to how your strengths can help you navigate challenges. When you appreciate what you do well, you're more likely to extend kindness and patience to yourself in moments of struggle.

Take a moment to reflect: What are you naturally good at? What qualities have helped you overcome past obstacles? What do people appreciate about you? Too often, you are quick to list your weaknesses but hesitant to acknowledge your superpowers. However, recognizing your strengths isn't arrogance—it's self-awareness.

Self-compassion means treating yourself with the same encouragement and grace that you would offer a friend. One way to practice this is by celebrating small wins. At the end of each day, instead of replaying mistakes, remind yourself of what you accomplished. Shifting your focus from what's missing to what's present helps you cultivate a more balanced and resilient mindset.

By leaning into your strengths with appreciation, you build the foundation for self-compassion. You stop seeing yourself through the lens of deficiency and start recognizing your own brilliance—allowing yourself to move forward with confidence and kindness.

Challenging Yourself with Self-Compassion In Your Day

Instead of comparing yourself to a self-imposed standard, focus on your own unique qualities and progress. Don't get attached to the idea of an "ideal" and instead strive to live life on your own terms. That is again, challenging yourself with self-compassion. It emerges as a powerful and transformative tool in pursuing a successful and fulfilling career, and it's a crucial step in the ABCD of Positive Self-Talk (Finish Chapter). Integrating self-compassion into your day-to-day self-talk will allow you to embrace imperfection and unlock your true potential. The following are some tips that can be helpful to be kind to yourself:

Be Your Best Friend

Think about what you would say to a friend about the situation. You are probably thinking about the worst outcome. What else could be possible? Your presentation could have been better, but it was not the worst, right?

What Else

Think about what else you can do besides worrying. Can you ask for support? Can you prepare better for the next presentation? Can you learn from what didn't go well?

Embrace Failure as a Learning Opportunity

Failure is an inevitable part of any career. Rather than attaching your self-worth to success or failure, view setbacks as valuable learning experiences. Understand that every failure brings an opportunity for growth, resilience, and personal development. Embracing failure with non-attachment allows you to bounce back stronger, learn from mistakes, and approach future endeavors with renewed determination, self-confidence and curiosity.

Practice "Sometimes" Thinking

Avoid absolutes like "I will always be" or "I will never be." Ph.D. Diana Hills[xxxix] recommends using sometimes instead, like "I am anxious, sometimes." "Sometimes" thinking can help you change your narrative and accept that you don't always perform the same; there is a context you cannot control. A good example is saying, "You're sometimes a good runner." When you're focused on self-as-content, you believe your mind's stories about who you are, like being a good runner. However, thinking of self-as-context, not self-as-content, is a more flexible way to observe yourself with open awareness and take multiple perspectives.

Practice Self-Forgiveness

Forgive yourself by normalizing your mistakes. What is the benefit of punishing yourself for long hours? Perfectionists remind themselves how bad they are, which keeps them stuck in the past and worried about making the same mistake in the future. Learn from mistakes, grow and move on.

Put Your Suffering In Perspective

Realizing that a mistake is not the end of the world and that there are always new opportunities can change your thinking. However, it is hard to think that way or accept mistakes until something meaningful helps you see them. Tennis player Roger Federer was a perfectionist who suffered with every defeat until his coach died. That event made him put winning in perspective: "Any defeat in tennis is nothing compared to such a moment."

Zoom Out

Zoom Out When you're feeling worried, it's easy to become fixated on the issue at hand, focusing all your energy on it. The next time you notice this, try zooming out—viewing the situation from a broader, more constructive perspective. Recall past moments when you were praised or felt proud of your accomplishments. Shifting your focus can help you regain perspective and approach the challenge with a clearer mind. Some practical ways to zoom out could be imagining yourself as a bird looking at the situation and observing yourself, for instance, you and your boss talking.

✦ PRO TIP: Ask yourself in the third person: What is Lucy feeling? What would Lucy say? What is the boss feeling?

Don't Take It Personally

When you internalize feedback or a failure, you place the entire burden of responsibility on yourself. While taking ownership of your actions is important, don't carry blame that isn't yours to shoulder.

Many people ask me, "How do I avoid taking it personally?" I know it's challenging—especially for those of us who tend to internalize everything. It's easy to think, *"I could have done better."* However, it's crucial to recognize that not everything is within your control. Yes, you can always look for ways to improve, but factors outside your influence affect the final result.

Taking things personally only increases worry and stress about others' perceptions of you. It can also trigger deep insecurities, reinforcing negative beliefs about your abilities. Instead of dwelling on what others might think or getting caught up in self-criticism, focus on solutions.

As a coach, I encourage people to take responsibility for their part but also urge them to acknowledge that perfection isn't the goal. Embrace your 50% (or whatever feels right for you), then channel your energy into moving forward.

If the feedback is about your performance, it's essential to separate the constructive feedback from your personal worth. Use it as an opportunity for growth, not self-blame. Remember, feedback—whether from a colleague, boss, or even family member—doesn't define you. They don't always have to be right. Decide what's actionable and what you can let go of.

If you're dealing with a mistake or failure, widen your perspective to include other factors that may have influenced the outcome. It's important to recognize that you are not the only one in the equation. Acknowledge your role, take corrective action, and move forward.

The Power of Narrowing Your Timeframe

Worries about the past or future can weigh heavily on our busy minds. When that happens, it's important to be intentional and focus on what you can do today. Timeboxing is a great tool for this, as it helps you narrow your timeframe and work in manageable chunks—like one hour at a time. Rather than thinking about how much you've already done or how much is left to do, stay present and focus on the process and progress. By doing so, you can reduce overthinking and increase productivity.

I remember a coachee who had recently been laid off. She was consumed by worries about how the layoff would appear on her resume. She started spiraling, thinking about what would happen if she couldn't find a job soon—would she have to move back in with her parents? What would she do with her clothes and furniture in a smaller space?

The key here was helping her focus on what she could control in the present moment, even within a short timeframe. She was already deep into the interview process with a major company, so the next step was clear: focus on preparing for the upcoming interviews, researching other opportunities, and presenting a confident narrative about her journey—even with the layoff.

Timeboxing these tasks would help her stay focused and break them down into manageable, less overwhelming steps. By allocating specific chunks of time to each task—like one hour for research or 30 minutes for refining her interview responses—she could move through each task with clarity and purpose.

We agreed that stressing about moving back with her parents wasn't productive right now. Based on her savings, we decided she could consider that in three months if necessary. For now, the focus was on what she could do to move forward.

Seek the Positive Intention

Behind every thought, no matter how negative or intrusive it may seem, lies a positive intention. Instead of dismissing or suppressing these thoughts, take the time to explore their underlying motivations. Are they trying to teach you a lesson, protect you from potential harm, or provide guidance for personal growth? By seeking the positive intention behind your thoughts, you can reframe them in a more constructive light.

Practice Non-attachment

Attachment, in psychological terms, refers to the emotional bond or connection we form with people, outcomes, or possessions. It can create a sense of security or reliance, but it can also lead to unhealthy dependency when we become overly attached to a specific outcome, object, or person. In the context of work, attachment can manifest as an intense fixation on a particular goal, promotion, or recognition to the point where your self-worth and happiness are deeply tied to these external outcomes.

Just as you learned how timeboxing helps you focus on one task at a time without letting thoughts and distractions mix together, practicing non-attachment involves setting clear mental boundaries. It means distinguishing who you are from the outcomes you achieve. Our worries and emotions can make things seem blurry and all mixed up together, but they don't have to be.

Cultivating non-attachment is a practice that requires intentional effort and ongoing self-awareness. Much like in personal relationships, having an insecure attachment to your work can lead to stress, anxiety, or disengagement, particularly if you become fixated on specific outcomes such as a salary increase, a promotion, or the approval of a manager. This type of attachment can lead to emotional burnout and dissatisfaction when expectations aren't met, making it harder to stay focused and productive.

However, non-attachment to expectations isn't about disengaging or showing indifference toward your work. Instead, it involves adopting a mindset that allows you to detach from rigid outcomes, recognizing that external achievements or recognition are only one part of the equation. You shift your focus to the present moment, fostering a deeper sense of fulfillment that comes from the process rather than the result.

This mindset allows you to engage fully in your work, appreciating the growth, challenges, and learning along the way. It encourages flexibility, so you remain open to new opportunities, even when things are unplanned. Non-attachment also helps you detach from the need to constantly prove your worth through external validation, such as job titles or promotions. By recognizing that external achievements do not solely define your self-worth, you create space for self-compassion and inner peace, fostering a healthier relationship with your career.

In practice, this means giving yourself permission to pursue your goals without expecting too much. It involves recognizing when you're investing too much energy into outcomes beyond your control and gently reminding yourself that your value is not tied to your work success. Ultimately, practicing non-attachment allows you to remain present and centered, focusing on what truly matters—growth, purpose, and fulfillment—rather than stressing over what you cannot control.

Sustaining Self-care

As you begin implementing strategies to combat multitasking, procrastination, perfectionism and other tendencies like people-pleasing, self-compassion becomes the cornerstone of this process. Self-care starts by recognizing your behavior patterns and making a conscious effort to shift from self-criticism to self-acceptance. Instead of overworking yourself to prove your worth, you set realistic expectations, take regular breaks, and create boundaries that protect your time and energy. It helps you perform at your best, prevents burnout, and fosters a healthier and sustainable relationship with work, your loved ones, and yourself.

Once you establish this internal balance, you can more effectively interact with your team, bringing that same sense of compassion to group dynamics.

Learn to RESET

R Relax
E Enjoy
S Simplify
E Exercise
T Thank

@lucypaulisecoach

Mastering time management and productivity isn't just about doing more—it's about resetting your mindset, energy, and habits to work *smarter* while maintaining wellbeing. Instead of letting stress accumulate, learning how to reset helps you regain clarity, sustain focus, and prevent burnout.

While introducing new stress-management techniques in the middle of a high-pressure situation can feel overwhelming, the best time to build a reset routine is *before* you need it—during less stressful moments like weekends or vacations. Developing these habits proactively will make it easier to apply them daily when work gets intense.

When stress builds up, your ability to focus, make decisions, and stay productive diminishes. Resetting doesn't mean checking out completely—it's about integrating small, intentional actions that help you pause, reflect, and regain energy throughout the day. The more you practice managing different situations, the more natural and effortless it becomes.

The RESET Framework: Five Habits for Energy & Performance

These five habits will help you **RESET**, enhance your performance, and find more joy at work:

1. **Relax** – Calm your mind by breathing deeply.
2. **Enjoy the Process with Compassion** – Shift your focus to positivity and growth rather than pressure and perfection.
3. **Simplify** – Reduce unnecessary clutter—mentally and physically.
4. **Exercise** – Move your body to improve focus and energy.
5. **Thank** – Cultivate gratitude for progress and support.

Relax: Calm Your Mind with Deep Breathing

Stress activates your body's fight-or-flight response, increasing blood pressure, heart rate, and cortisol levels. While short-term stress can boost focus and memory, excessive stress leads to overwhelm and reduced performance—making it harder to speak clearly, make quick decisions, or even recognize when you're stressed.

To reset your stress response, practice relaxation techniques daily, not just when you feel overwhelmed. Just 10 minutes of deep breathing can help calm your nervous system, regain control, and increase mental clarity. The more you practice, the easier it becomes to shift into a relaxed state when needed.

✦ PRO TIP: Start with a simple breathing exercise— inhale for four counts, hold for four, exhale for four and hold again for four.

Enjoy the Process with Compassion: Shift to Positivity & Growth

Once your body is calm, you gain more control over your thoughts. As I mentioned before, a common challenge in high-achievers is negative self-talk, often fueled by comparison, self-doubt, or fear of failure.

If your manager doesn't respond to an email or you're excluded from a meeting, your mind might jump to negative conclusions: *Did I do something wrong? Am I being left out?* This is counterproductive thinking that increases stress and reduces motivation.

Instead of focusing on what went wrong, shift to what's going well. Practicing self-compassion and celebrating small wins helps build resilience and prevents burnout.

✦ PRO TIP: At the end of each day, think of one thing you are proud of. This helps rewire your brain to recognize progress instead of only focusing on what's unfinished.

Simplify: Reduce Clutter & Focus on What Matters

A cluttered environment—whether physical or mental—creates decision fatigue and distraction.

Physically: Take a look at your workspace—how many unnecessary papers, emails, or apps are adding to your stress? Mentally: How many unnecessary tasks, perfectionist tendencies, or self-imposed pressures are draining your energy?

To simplify your workday, reduce unnecessary inputs, streamline your to-do list, and focus only on tasks that truly align with your priorities.

✦ PRO TIP: Try the "Do Later Parking Lot"—if a task isn't urgent or essential, write it down and revisit it when you have more capacity, rather than letting it hijack your focus.

Exercise: Move to Reset Your Mind

Overthinking can trap you in stress mode, making it harder to focus. Engaging in physical movement helps reset your brain by shifting attention from stress to body awareness. Walk, run, or stretch—even five minutes can reduce stress hormones. Try a mind-body activity like yoga or mindful movement to release tension. Use movement to process emotions—many great ideas come during a walk or workout because they allow space for creative problem-solving.

✦ PRO TIP: If you're feeling stuck or overwhelmed, take a 5-minute movement break before returning to your task. You'll come back with fresh energy.

Thank: Cultivate Gratitude & Acknowledge Progress

Stress often stems from excessive demands and the fear of not doing enough. One of the most powerful ways to reset is to appreciate progress and support. Acknowledge what you've achieved—even small steps matter. Thank your team— recognition boosts motivation and team morale, and thank yourself too. Practice gratitude daily—before bed, reflect on one thing you're grateful for that day.

If you feel like nothing went right, you're being too hard on yourself. Try again. Even the smallest positive moment counts.

✦ PRO TIP: Use the "Losada Ratio"—for every negative thought, identify three positive ones.

RESET isn't about avoiding stress—it's about managing it with intention and compassion. The more you practice these habits daily, the easier it will be to reset when you need it most. Instead of getting stuck in frustration, overthinking, or exhaustion, these small shifts will help you stay focused, energized, and in control.

Reset Your Burnout Levels

People with burnout complain that they have to do 6-week work in 3 weeks, that they work until late at night or can't stop thinking about work when they sleep or in the shower. Can you reset burnout? How can you even prevent it? Burnout is a chronic imbalance between your job demands and your job resources.

It's often correlated with anxiety and depression and predicts other mental health challenges. For example, those who feel tense or stressed out during the workday are more than three times as likely[xl] to seek employment elsewhere.

The challenge to reduce burnout or tackle it before it gets worse is that when you most need to recover, you're least likely to engage in recovery activities because you are already overwhelmed and in a vicious cycle that doesn't allow you to change your behaviors or ask for help.

While some drivers of burnout could be a toxic culture or a micro-manager, focus on what you can control first:

Shape your environment for optimal recovery.

Keep your space free of distractions. Remove work-related stuff from your sight during your free time. Your mind will focus on what is available, so if you want to relax, close the door to your home office, travel somewhere even if it is one hour away, or walk in nature. Staying outside in the sun or spending more time in rooms with good natural light can help recharge.

Learn which triggers prevent you from psychologically detaching from work.

If that includes your phone or computer, then go for it. For example, turn off notifications temporarily or do not take the work phone with you everywhere.

Choose to replace work with an activity that you enjoy.

Reading, running, or cooking allows you to focus entirely or stay in flow and mentally disconnect your thoughts of work. If you are doing an activity you don't genuinely enjoy just to share with someone, you may not feel wholly involved and go back to thinking about work. Try to choose something special for you intentionally.

Choose high-effort recovery activities.

Harvard Business Review[xli] recommends that "While it may seem that relaxing, watching TV, or other "passive" or "low-effort" activities are best for recovery, on the contrary, research shows that more active activities can be even more effective for recovery." Pursuing a hobby that requires effort or mastery, like learning a new language or skill, helps you stay in flow for more prolonged, replenish depleted resources, and have an optimal experience outside work. It is also a good reminder that work is not the only way to have some fun.

Brain Dump

Another tool to reset your burnout is the brain dump, the process of unloading thoughts, worries, tasks, and ideas onto paper or a digital tool—without organizing or filtering them. The goal is to clear your mind. By decluttering your thoughts, you free up mental bandwidth and gain a clearer perspective on your priorities.

This practice is beneficial during challenging times, as writing down your thoughts encourages self-reflection and provides a sense of relief. It helps shift your brain from a heightened state of stress or anxiety, governed by the amygdala, into a more reflective and calm state, reducing stress, managing to overthink and boosting productivity and clarity to solve problems more creatively.

A great time to perform a brain dump is when you are starting a complex project. Many people feel paralyzed when beginning a massive project at work, with dozens of emails and timelines ahead. A brain dump helps you put all those tasks in one place, easing your sense of overwhelm and giving you a clear starting point.

Many people use brain dumping also as part of their nighttime routine to ensure all day's worries are put to rest.

Jotting down to-dos and thoughts just before bed can improve your sleep quality, allowing you to wake up refreshed.

It can be a great help when you're working on a creative project and feel stuck. A brain dump can help you break through the block. You may uncover new connections and inspiration by writing down all your ideas, even those that seem irrelevant or unpolished.

How to Perform a Brain Dump

1. **Choose Your Medium**: Decide whether you prefer pen and paper or a digital tool. Both methods have their advantages. Writing by hand can be therapeutic and help you process emotions. Research[xlii] shows that it deepens content processing and supports emotional health. On the other hand, digital tools allow for easy editing, categorization, and integration into your workflow. Choose the method that feels most natural and effective for you.

2. **Write Freely**: Jot down everything that comes to mind—tasks, worries, ideas, or random thoughts. Don't worry about grammar, structure, or prioritization.

3. **Type of Writing:** Depending on the kind of worry or thoughts you are having, you can either write a paragraph or list items. For instance, if you are worried about one particular matter and need to process it, writing a paragraph may help you reflect and gain clarity. If you are concerned about several tasks that need to get done the next day, listing them as a to-do list may be more effective in organizing your actions.

4. **Review and Organize**: Once you're done, review your list. Identify actionable tasks, group similar ideas, and highlight priorities. This step transforms your brain dump into a practical tool. If you are in the middle of the night, you can leave this step for later when you wake up.

5. **Make It a Habit**: Incorporate brain dumps into your routine, such as at the start or end of the day or whenever you feel overwhelmed. Establishing a habit strengthens neural pathways through repetition, known as neuroplasticity, making self-reflection and emotional processing more accessible over time. Make it easy for yourself by keeping your preferred medium nearby. For instance, I always have a pen and paper on my bedside table, which prevents turning on my phone.

A brain dump is a simple yet transformative technique for managing stress, reducing overthinking, and boosting productivity. Additionally, by making a habit, the anticipation of journaling provides a dopamine release, enhancing motivation and a sense of accomplishment. In a world that often demands perfection and constant mental activity, this practice reminds us to pause, reflect, and declutter. Whether facing a busy workday or wrestling with life's complexities, a brain dump can be our go-to strategy for achieving mental clarity and focus.

Vacation or Workation?

Balancing work and personal life in the modern world is becoming more challenging. Many people choose to go on vacation to RESET, but then "workation" happens - combining work and vacation time.

Workations allow flexibility in mixing work and leisure activities, but it's important to find a balance and avoid overworking during time off.

While many people argue that you should not work during holidays, the advantage is that it allows you to go out more often without impacting your job stability or the total hours worked during the month. The negative side of workation is feeling guilty or worried while not working.

Workations should complement paid time off but not serve as a substitute.

Here, I share the advantages of workations and offer tips on keeping work from taking over your relaxation time.

Embracing the Workation Concept

Workations are the perfect solution for professionals who want to work from unique and inspiring locations and break free from the traditional office environment. By combining work with vacation, individuals can explore new destinations, travel more, and rejuvenate while fulfilling their work commitments. This approach enhances productivity and creativity and promotes overall wellbeing by eliminating the boundaries between work and personal life.

Setting Boundaries and Prioritizing Rest

While workations offer flexibility, it is crucial to establish clear boundaries to ensure a healthy work-life balance. Start by setting specific working hours and designating time for relaxation and personal activities. By prioritizing rest, you allow yourself the opportunity to recharge and fully enjoy the vacation aspect of your work. Communicate these boundaries with colleagues and clients, making it clear that certain hours are dedicated solely to personal time.

Before embarking on a workation, create a schedule for both work and leisure activities. Set realistic goals and allocate specific time slots for work-related tasks. Planning your workload in advance ensures that work stays within your vacation time. Avoid having work so scattered that you feel there is no time off.

Embracing Mindfulness and Disconnecting

Disconnecting can be more difficult depending on the type of work you do. By turning off notifications, checking email / Slack and phones at specific times and setting "do not disturb," you can use technology to help you draw a line and focus on one thing at a time. Practice a shutdown routine every day you work.

Delegating and Collaborating

Delegate tasks and responsibilities whenever possible, ensuring that colleagues or team members can step in when needed. Effective collaboration can help distribute workload, reduce stress, and prevent the need for excessive work during holidays. By fostering a culture of trust and teamwork, you can rely on others to handle certain tasks while you enjoy your workation.

Let Go Guilt

One last piece of advice is to let go of the guilt[xliii] and embrace the joy of going on holiday. Taking a break and exploring new places is a well-deserved treat and a vital aspect of self-care. You work hard and deserve to enjoy. Vacations offer an opportunity to recharge, relax, and gain new perspectives. So, instead of feeling guilty, embrace the excitement and adventure of planning and embarking on a holiday. If you hear that voice inside you that urges you to be "on" all the time to be accepted, tell yourself it is OK to be off and allow yourself to stay disconnected. Remind yourself that success comes from focusing on the progress you are making every year, not on driving outstanding results every day.

Ask For What You Need

While the tips I have shared so far can help you improve your self-care, it's equally important to communicate with your coworkers and let them know your needs. Discuss what you require and how they can offer support, and make sure to take regular breaks to recharge.

Whether from managers, colleagues, friends, or family, asking for help opens the door to fresh perspectives and solutions that may help you move forward more confidently. It can also relieve some of the mental burden, allowing you to regain clarity and confidence in your decisions.

When asking for help, try to ask specific, targeted questions to ensure you're aligned with what truly needs your attention. For example, "What do you think is the most important next step in this project?" or "Can you share your perspective on how I can simplify this decision?" By seeking input, you're not only clarifying your next steps but also reinforcing your own abilities and confidence by making more informed choices.

Remember, seeking help isn't a reflection of inadequacy—it's a powerful tool for improving your focus and decision-making. It's about leveraging the strengths and insights of others to complement your own, ultimately helping you stay on track and achieve your goals more effectively.

Speak up if you have specific needs—whether you're neurodiverse, experiencing anxiety, feeling burned out, or simply exhausted from the day. Your wellbeing matters, and advocating for the right support can make all the difference. While you increase your self-awareness, you may discover that some places are better for you to work than others. Be comfortable asking for what you want from your boss or your family. Give yourself permission to explore and understand your own needs or follow what your doctor recommends if applicable. Be kind to yourself. What you need could be from DO NOT DISTURB moments, where you block your calendar or turn off notifications, to reminders and apps to help you prioritize what is more urgent. Frequent check-ins with your manager or your partner can also help clarify expectations about what to focus on first.

Team Compassion

Self-compassion is not limited to how you treat yourself; it also extends to how you interact with others in the workplace. By developing self-compassion, you become more understanding and empathetic toward your colleagues. You are less likely to engage in harsh judgments or criticisms and more open to offering support.

Once you've started practicing self-compassion, the next step is to extend that compassion to your team or colleagues. Just as you've worked to reduce self-imposed stress, fostering a work environment that encourages mutual care and understanding is equally important. Compassionate leadership and teamwork play critical roles in this.

As a leader or team member, you must be mindful of how your team manages its time workload. Additionally, consider how they might be affected by imposter syndrome and its byproducts, such as perfectionism and procrastination. Compassionate leadership means recognizing these challenges and supporting your team through them.

Here are some key ways to nurture compassion within your team:

1. **Encourage Open Communication:** Create an environment where team members feel safe to express their challenges without fear of judgment. Be transparent about your own struggles to foster trust and build a culture of vulnerability.

2. **Promote Flexibility:** Ensure there's room for flexibility within your timeboxing system. Set realistic deadlines, allow time for decompression, and be mindful of your team's emotional and mental wellbeing.

3. **Acknowledge Struggles:** Recognize when someone might be struggling with feelings of inadequacy or stress. Support can make a significant difference in how they engage with their work.

4. **Foster Collaboration and Shared Problem-Solving:** Timeboxing isn't just a productivity tool—it can also serve as a way to ensure that everyone on the team is moving forward together. When workloads are distributed relatively, and team members feel supported, they are more likely to engage fully and bring their best selves to the workplace.

Combining self-care with team care creates a balanced approach that supports personal growth and collective success. Compassion becomes the foundation for a high-performing, supportive team culture.

The Impact of Surrounding Relationships

As you develop a time management routine, you'll notice how your behaviors and routines are influenced not only by your internal beliefs but also by the expectations of those around you—your team, family, and peers. The environment and relationships surrounding you significantly affect how you manage your time and handle stress.

Now that you've established a personal routine, the next step is teaching timeboxing with compassion to your team. By implementing practices that benefit you and those you work with, you create an environment of mutual support, empathy, and shared responsibility. This approach encourages everyone to feel valued and ensures that no one bears the weight of unrealistic expectations alone.

By fostering this compassionate culture, you lay the groundwork for an empowered team that collaborates, thrives, and manages time with intention and understanding.

Help Your Team Prioritize

A Microsoft report[xliv] shows that 81% of employees say it's vital that their managers help them prioritize their workload, but less than a third (31%) say their managers have ever given clear guidance during one-on-ones. Helping your team prioritize work, whether you are an official leader or not, can also help reduce stress and prevent burnout. When team members are overwhelmed with too many tasks, they may feel anxious and stressed, reducing productivity and decreasing morale, which are contagious. By helping your team prioritize their work, you can help alleviate their and your stress and ensure everyone can focus on what matters the most.

Use a shared task-management system to enhance communication, transparency, and accountability. If you use a personal kanban or an app that helps you stay organized, discuss with your team what could work for all of you and help them get started with the same tools. Ask what they need to succeed continuously, especially if it feels like the work is not moving forward, and regularly review and adjust priorities together.

Learn to Say "No"

Saying "no" to your boss and anyone is a challenge for many of us. We often overextend ourselves due to people-pleasing, fear of missing out, or underestimating how much time tasks will take. Modern work cultures encourage collaboration and helping others while simultaneously pushing the idea of continuous growth by adding new responsibilities. This often makes us feel guilty for saying no or declining a meeting, but it also leads to our days being never-ending. These tendencies can result in burnout, decreased productivity, and an inability to focus on the work that truly matters.

To manage this, take the time to assess each request carefully. Ask yourself whether you can realistically take it on and when you can complete it. Set clear rules for yourself, like a personal compass, to guide your decision-making. Establish boundaries, such as not accepting new tasks after certain hours or delegating work outside your area of expertise. Saying "no" strategically helps protect your time and energy, allowing you to focus on high-priority tasks that align with your goals.

Clarifying expectations is key. Ask questions to fully understand what's being asked and how much time it will require. Be upfront about your boundaries so others know what to expect. Developing the ability to set boundaries and intentionally decide how to use your time allows you to balance collaboration, growth, and self-care.

One reason we often say "yes" is the emotional relief it provides by avoiding potential conflict. However, rather than seeing it as conflict, reframe the conversation as an honest evaluation of whether you're the best person for the task. If you can't meet the deadline or lack the necessary expertise, your honest feedback might be more helpful than forcing a "yes." By being upfront, you create an opportunity to collaborate and find the best way forward.

The Spectrum of "No": From "No" to "Yes, But"

Learning to say "no" doesn't have to be a hard line. There are various ways to decline or set boundaries while still offering value. Consider the following spectrum:

1. **No:**
   Use this when the request clearly doesn't align with your priorities or workload. For example, "I'm currently focused on other projects and can't take this on right now" or "This isn't within my area of expertise."

2. **Yes, but...**
   If the request is important but requires boundaries, this is a great option. For example, "Yes, but I can only dedicate an hour to this project, so I won't be able to deliver the full scope" or "I can't handle this entire task, but I'm happy to assist with a portion."

3. **It depends, can you tell me more?**
   This is helpful when you need to assess if the task fits within your priorities. You could say, "Yes, maybe—let me check my schedule and get back to you," or ask for clarification on which parts of the task are most urgent.

Managing Meetings and Emails

Saying "no" also applies to meetings, emails, and events. Studies show that more than 85% of employees' time[xlv] is spent in meetings, and half of those meetings are unproductive. Similarly, with email management, if you're constantly copied on emails that don't concern you, consider asking to be removed, unsubscribing, or using AI tools to clean your inbox.

Before agreeing to any meetings, ask yourself:

- Are you the right person to attend, or can someone else handle it?
- Is the meeting necessary, or could the issue be addressed via email or a phone call?
- Does the meeting have a clear objective and agenda?
- Does the timing make sense, given your current priorities?

When you say no to tasks that don't align with your core responsibilities, you are saying yes to being more productive, focused, and valuable. It's not about being unhelpful; it's about protecting your time and energy so you can do your best work.

Takeaways

- **Self-compassion:** The practice of being kind, understanding, and patient with oneself during times of failure, struggle, or difficulty rather than being self-critical.

- **Team compassion:** The ability to show empathy, understanding, and support for team members, fostering a culture of care, respect, and encouragement within the group.

- **RESET:** A method or strategy to pause, reflect, and realign thoughts and actions with a compassionate and centered mindset, especially when overwhelmed or stressed.

- **Self-forgiveness:** The act of releasing guilt, regret, or blame toward oneself, recognizing mistakes as part of the human experience and allowing oneself to move forward without self-punishment.

- **Self-care:** Intentional actions and practices that prioritize one's physical, emotional, and mental wellbeing, ensuring balance and resilience.

- **Brain dump:** A technique of unloading all thoughts, ideas, and tasks onto paper or digital tools to reduce mental clutter, clarify priorities, and create space for focus.

- **Strengths:** Innate abilities, skills, and talents that individuals possess, which can be leveraged to improve performance, build confidence, and achieve goals.

- **Non-attachment:** The practice of letting go of excessive attachment to outcomes, material possessions, or expectations, allowing for greater peace and freedom in navigating life's challenges.

Practical Tips to Cultivate Self-Care With Compassion

RESET
Practice RESET every day at work, especially when you feel overwhelmed, to enhance your performance and find more joy at work:

Relax – Calm your mind by breathing deeply.

Enjoy the Process with Compassion – Shift your focus to positivity and growth rather than pressure and perfection.

Simplify – Reduce unnecessary clutter—mentally and physically.

Exercise – Move your body to improve focus and energy.

Thank – Cultivate gratitude for progress and support.

Shine on your strengths.
To practice more compassion, start by acknowledging and embracing your strengths, especially when you find yourself idealizing the strengths of others. Instead of fixating on perceived shortcomings or areas where you feel less capable, focus on how your strengths can help you navigate challenges. When you recognize and appreciate what you excel at, you create a foundation of self-assurance and positivity. This mindset makes it easier to extend kindness and patience to yourself during moments of struggle, fostering resilience and self-compassion in the process.

Download the worksheet for this chapter at
www.lucypaulise.com/timebox

Chapter 9 | FOLLOW UP
It's Time To Shine

How to Measure Success with Compassion

"I feel empowered now"

"[I realized] my weaknesses were weakened. This process made me believe and regain my desire to move forward, to look at life and work situations from another point of view, expand my vision and put myself in the place of the other. Since I took her sessions, my work life has changed radically. I can only thank Lucy for helping me to move forward in a positive way."

As you can see by reading the previous chapters, failing to manage your time is not like a genetic trait, something that you cannot change. While some genetic and environmental factors can make it more challenging to succeed in managing your time, getting better at it is the result of strategy and discipline.

As I was writing this book, I reached a point where I felt utterly stuck. I knew exactly what I wanted to say, but despite my best intentions, I couldn't find the time or motivation to get to work and finish it. It baffled me because I felt I should know better as the author of a time management book. But as a coach, I also recognized that something deeper was at play. What I was facing wasn't just a lack of time or discipline—it was exhaustion.

The drive to finish the book pushed me beyond my limits without considering how I felt. The many things simultaneously demanding my attention left me tired, stressed, and overwhelmed. In this moment of struggle, I realized the importance of the book's final part: the need for self-compassion. It was clear that I had to give myself the grace I so often encourage others to practice.

As you can imagine, it is not just me. Buenout is real. A Gallup report[xlvi] shows that about three in four employees in the U.S. experience workplace burnout at least sometimes, and about one in four experience burnout either "very often" or "always." Burnout often happens because of an extended period of chronic stress at work, including working long hours, having too much on your plate, and feeling out of control.

Peter Drucker would say, "We can't manage what we can't measure." So, measure how you are doing if you want to manage your time better. Can you review every day, at the end of the day, what worked well about your day and what did not work so well?

Evaluate results by asking the following questions:
- Which tasks take longer than expected?
- Which tasks are unplanned?
- Which tasks could be reduced?
- Which tasks could be delegated?

• Were there any extra costs?

If your schedule works well, repeat the same routine: consistent practice produces mastery and makes for new habits.

If things are not going well and you feel too tired to evaluate your day, pay attention to your feelings the following day. Try to identify your red and green tasks, what energizes you and what drains you.

Once you've become aware of how you manage your time and how it impacts your wellbeing, it is time to start practicing self-care, primarily through compassion.

At the beginning of the year, you evaluate your performance and consider your future goals. Unfortunately, you may set yourself up for a chronic stress condition. If your goals are unrealistic or your bar is set too high, the pace at which you tackle your to-do list can drive burnout, resignation or internal frustration.

Finding a way to evaluate your year more positively based on progress, not outcome, can help you avoid being too hard on yourself, celebrate small wins and redefine progress in the upcoming year to prevent stress and burnout.

The Impact Of Focusing Too Much On Results

The main problem of focusing on results lies in judging your worth based on achieving a particular promotion, earning a certain amount, or reaching a specific goal in a specific period. Even though very typical, all these things can be out of your control. No matter how well you perform, there will always be exceptional circumstances you cannot predict, impacting your final results. While you may have made much effort or progress towards your goal, you may not see it. In your mind (or your supervisors'), defining these goals more objectively could make sense to evaluate your performance. But, in the end, it could make you feel frustrated and set the wrong state of mind for what is next.

Budgets, problem-solving metrics, and analytics keep our brain more in the NEA state (negative emotional attractor). We need the NEA to solve problems, analyze, make decisions, and focus. While the NEA is required to move a person from vision to action, research[xlvii] shows that a person must spend significantly more time in the positive state of mind PEA to achieve sustained desired change.

In his book Helping People Change[xlviii], Richard Boyatzis states that overemphasizing results or what "should be" causes people to operate in a negative state of fight-or-flight, fear, and anxiety. As a result, they become more closed to sharing and more focused on being defensive than interacting positively, and they shut down the capacity to change, learn or even plan realistically.

Reward Progress, Not Outcomes

When you focus on your progress—what you have done so far—rather than what is missing, your PEA (positive state) is turned on, and you shine. Your eyes get brighter, and your speech gets faster. You will be more open to possibilities and feel renewed and curious.

To focus on progress, trust, and stick to the process rather than continuously adjusting to find a specific result. Just like you learned to do with tasks, you can divide the process into smaller steps or milestones to see progress even when a complete goal is not achieved (remember we talked about celebrating partial success, too).

Comparisons are your worst enemy. Do not take rankings, salaries or promotions as a measure of your worth; they are just labels. Instead, evaluate how aligned your progress is to your purpose and celebrate even baby steps as long as they are in the right direction. You have more chances to succeed in the long term when you focus on your journey and growth areas. In the long term, everything can be possible even when now seems impossible. Be patient when deadlines aren't attainable and flexible to redefine what is possible in the current situation. The goal, again, is to make progress.

By celebrating progress, no matter how small, you can feel more confident to evaluate where you are more often, adjust your goals or action items, and, more importantly, enjoy the journey. Embracing your present as is, not judging it or expecting it to be different, helps you be more compassionate with yourself, creative about overcoming issues, and engage in more healthy and positive self-talk.

✦ PRO TIP: By the end of the day, don't get stuck obsessing over what went wrong. Be thankful for all the tasks accomplished.

Turning New Year's Resolutions Into Daily Habits

"It's already mid-January, and I struggle to keep up with my New Year's resolution."

I often hear this concern. Don't worry—you're not alone. It is a common experience for many people every year. While it's tempting to set resolutions, and even schools encourage teens to do so, it's essential to consider how realistic they are. Can you truly achieve them?

The key is choosing resolutions that can be seamlessly integrated into your daily routine, avoiding the frustration of unrealistic expectations. You don't have to alter the resolution completely; instead, you can redefine it to make it more achievable and aligned with your schedule. Follow the steps you learn to timebox, focus, flow, and finish.

Below are some practical strategies for turning your New Year's resolutions into effortless daily habits that will positively impact your career.

Focus

As you have learned in previous chapters, prioritize what is most essential for you and break down your goals into daily actions.

Set two or three clear goals for the year and write down why achieving them matters to you. Who do you want to become once you've completed these goals? Can you connect them to North Star, guiding you throughout the year? As I shared in previous chapters, finding your North Star (or *ikigai*) can help you make better resolutions and decisions.

Choose your vital few goals, 2 or 3 goals (20% of your tasks that will give you 80% of your results) that will align with

Like walking down a forest, you can see the big mountain far ahead, but you need to focus on the immediate surroundings first.

Now, identify small, achievable steps rather than attempting drastic changes simultaneously. For example, if you aim to increase productivity, dedicate 15 minutes each morning to your highest-priority tasks. Similarly, if you want to begin exercising, instead of committing to an hour-long workout twice a week, start with 15 minutes of movement every day. You can't plan everything now. How do you cross any rivers ahead if you don't know where they are or what they look like? Plan, observe and adjust day by day. Once you take your first steps, you will discover what else is needed to get closer to your North Star.

Anchor Habits to Existing Routines

To form new habits, it can be helpful to link them to existing ones. Connect the new behavior you want to adopt with a current habit to make the transition smoother. For instance, if reading more is your goal, consider timeboxing it after dinner as part of your family time. Alternatively, you can listen to audiobooks during your commute.

Make It Easy

Make it as easy as possible to incorporate new habits into your day. Here are a few tips:

- **Start-up Time:** Choose activities (like exercise) that require little preparation or are easy to do at home. If preparation is necessary, streamline the process to make it quicker.
- **Frequency:** The more frequently you engage in the activity, the more likely it is to become a habit. If necessary, break the activity into smaller chunks, but maintain consistency.
- **Circadian Rhythm:** Identify the best time of day to perform your chosen activity. Some people prefer to exercise in the morning, while others opt for midday or evening workouts. Experiment and see what works best for you.
- **Variety** helps maintain interest and prevent boredom. I enjoy different forms of exercise, such as tennis, swimming, skating, and biking. For days I can't go outside, I have a home workout routine that focuses on core exercises. Variety keeps things exciting and helps me avoid excuses.
- **Size:** If you want to reduce your screen time or food consumption, you don't need to eliminate them.

Instead, focus on moderation. For example, reduce portion sizes or swap out some ingredients.

- **Lead Time:** Account for all the time required to adopt a habit, including prep and wrap-up. For instance, if you plan to start running, don't just consider the 30 minutes of running time—factor in the time to get dressed, hydrate, and shower afterward. Timeboxing everything makes your planning more realistic.

Stay Curious

When hiking, you don't need to see the entire path. You can simply follow the trail as it unfolds. Similarly, embrace the journey of your career. Stay open to unexpected opportunities and be prepared to adjust your course as you gain new insights and experiences. Avoid getting attached to your ideals or other people's expectations. Embrace and appreciate where you are getting at, and keep walking. This fluid approach allows for a more dynamic and fulfilling progression without the overwhelming feeling of attaching to a specific result. Think about your previous experiences and how often you did not get what you wanted but got a better fit.

Just as a hiker observes the changing landscapes in a forest, stay attuned to the shifts in your industry and workplace. Regularly evaluate your goals and adapt your plan based on new information. This mindfulness ensures that you remain agile and responsive to the evolving demands of your professional environment. Be curious and open to the unknown and to learn.

Be Consistent

Consistency is key when forming habits. Through timeboxing, you can make it easier to remember when to do what. Most importantly, don't be discouraged if you miss a day due to unexpected events. Use affirmations, set reminders, or enlist a coach as an accountability partner. The next day is always another opportunity to try again—and you can always make it easier if needed.

Transforming New Year's resolutions into lasting habits is a journey that requires commitment, patience, and intentionality. By starting with your goals in mind, you can turn your resolutions into lifelong habits that propel your career to new heights throughout the year.

Year-end Reflection

New Year Resolutions are good but worthless if there are no reflections. Most companies ask employees to do this type of review formally, so here are some tips to consider when doing yours. You might be thinking about whether you have achieved the goals you set for yourself. While constructive self-criticism can help you learn and improve, it's essential to be realistic and assertive about your goals for the following year. Whether you're getting ready for your year-end performance review or doing your annual personal reflection, it's crucial to celebrate your accomplishments, assess what didn't work out, and set a positive tone for the upcoming year.

End-of-year planning is a crucial phase for personal and career development. Realistically assessing how you wrapped up the year will set the foundation for a realistic start to your planning for the upcoming year. So, take some time to reflect and make it right. Create a personalized document to remind yourself what you have done, considering the following items:

Reflect on Achievements and Challenges

Begin your end-of-year career planning by reflecting on your achievements and challenges over the past months. What milestones have you reached? What projects stand out? Assessing your accomplishments provides a foundation for setting realistic and impactful goals for the upcoming year. Also, review the books you have read, the courses and webinars you have attended, and the coaching sessions you have had. All of them are signs of growth, effort and consistency.

Practice self-compassion

Take a moment to reflect on your accomplishments again from a self-compassionate perspective. Recall other achievements that may not have been grandiose but were significant enough for you to remember. Consider how much you have grown after facing challenges and craft a narrative that includes all your beautiful experiences. If there are things you wish were different, focus on things that are within your control and identify what you can do better next year. Write them down. Remember, they don't need to cloud your vision. You still have a lot to be thankful for. Hug yourself and tap on your self-confidence!

Prepare your performance review

If your organization conducts year-end performance reviews, prepare for them proactively. Take the time to document your achievements, contributions, and areas of improvement confidently. It is not the time to be humble. Instead, it is the perfect opportunity to showcase, with facts and metrics, how much you contributed to the organization and its impact on other organizations.

Assess your work-life balance

Review your work-life balance and make necessary changes to align with your personal and professional priorities. This could involve setting clear boundaries, delegating tasks, or exploring flexible work arrangements. To be more intentional next year, consider incorporating timeboxing into your daily routine. Additionally, it's worth evaluating your diet and exercise routines to determine if there are ways to take better care of yourself that you may have overlooked.

End-of-year planning is a crucial investment in your professional growth. Remember, it is not only about identifying what's missing but also about celebrating what went well. Seek out mentorship or coaching opportunities to help evaluate your performance. Many people struggle to assess their work due to shyness or perfectionism. Professional guidance and support can provide a fresh perspective and help you end the year positively. Celebrate where you are, and get ready to start another fantastic year!

Keeping up with the routines and tips you have learned so far is like a muscle; it has to be trained.

It's time to shine by training the time management muscle, maintaining a productive and balanced life.

Bonus Tips To Save Even More Time

Implement the "Inbox Zero" Method

When checking emails, act on them immediately to minimize clutter in your inbox. Use your designated "check email" time to implement the Inbox Zero method. It doesn't mean checking emails continuously but dedicating specific time to address each email intentionally with a follow-up action. Use the 4 Ds: Do Now, Do Later, Delegate, Delete. Consider using mailbox cleaning apps like Sanebox[xlix] to help you. The goal is to have no unread or pending emails by the end of the day or, at the latest, by the end of the week.

- **Do Now:**
  - ○ **Urgent emails:** Respond immediately to any email that requires action or attention.
  - ○ **Short emails:** If an email requires two or three minutes to respond to, don't leave it for later. Address it quickly. You can also create email templates to make it easier.
- **Do Later:**
  - ○ **Mark important emails as tasks:** if the email is important and requires more of your time and you cannot do it now, timebox some time to work on it later, or add it to your task list with a due date and mark it as read.
- **Delegate:** Don't let it sit in your inbox if you receive an email that you think will be better handled by a colleague, need to ask a question, or need to involve someone else before replying. Forward it or copy the person and pose the question immediately.

- **Delete:**
  - **Delete or mark as read:** As soon as you read an email that appears unimportant, delete it or mark it as read immediately.
  - **Reduce Unnecessary Emails:** Whether you are part of email chains that are not important to you or receiving too much spam, avoid the hassle by requesting to be removed from these chains or unsubscribing. You would be surprised to notice how much time you lose reading and deleting these emails.

Clean Up Your Mail Inbox

Managing your email inbox can be overwhelming due to the constant flow of messages, newsletters, and notifications. It's easy for your inbox to become cluttered. A well-organized inbox saves time, reduces stress, and increases productivity.

Avoiding Unnecessary Emails

The first step in cleaning up your inbox is reducing unnecessary emails before they arrive. When you receive unwanted promotional emails, classify them as spam or unsubscribe from mailing lists you no longer wish to follow.

Next, examine your work emails honestly. Consider how many are relevant to your role and whether they require immediate attention. Before relying on automated filters or tools, manually assess whether you need to be included in each email and meeting thread. If the content is irrelevant, request removal from the distribution list.

If a colleague or direct report could better handle the email, delegate it. Furthermore, explore alternative communication methods that avoid long email chains, like using Slack for quick exchanges or adding discussion topics to your next team meeting agenda. Streamlining communication and eliminating unnecessary messages will reduce inbox clutter and daily workflow noise.

After manually filtering your emails, you can use email tools or filters to prioritize important messages automatically. You can utilize Artificial Intelligence tools, such as Sanebox, to sort essential emails from unimportant ones and move them to appropriate folders, helping you organize your inbox.

Once you've cleared the unnecessary clutter, your primary inbox should mostly contain important emails. It will allow you to focus on urgent and essential matters when you're short on time. Check your crucial emails during natural breaks, and then check less critical emails only once a day.

Use Folders to Organize Your Inbox

Creating a folder system can significantly enhance your email management. Here are a few folder ideas to help you get started:

- **To-do:** Some emails that you receive may require you to take action. If you can reply in less than two minutes, do so immediately. If you need more time to work on it, move it to a to-do folder or use a tool like Google Tasks to mark the email to be added to your to-do list.
- **Spam and Unwanted Emails:** Create a folder to send emails you never want to see again. It is ideal for newsletters, advertisements, or any recurring spam. Set it up so that emails in this folder are automatically deleted after 30 days.
- **Receipts and Invoices:** Set up a folder for purchase receipts, invoices, and other transaction-related emails. Include emails related to family, work, and deliveries. It's an easy way to keep track of your spending and find important documents when needed.

- **Newsletters and Updates:** Direct all these emails to a specific folder if you subscribe to multiple newsletters or updates. You can find and read them conveniently without cluttering your primary inbox.
- **Non-Urgent Emails:** Create a folder for emails that aren't urgent and can be dealt with later.

Clear Out Old and Unnecessary Emails

Clear out old and unnecessary emails if you run out of storage space in your inbox. Summarize by email count and total attachment size, and start deleting or archiving emails that you no longer need. It frees up space and makes finding the emails that truly matter easier. To make it easier, schedule a monthly or bi-monthly cleaning time.

You can keep your email inbox clean and manageable by identifying and eliminating unnecessary emails, prioritizing essential messages, and organizing them with folders. Remember to clear out old emails regularly and set up automated rules to maintain this organization. Most importantly, remember that you can prevent email clutter by removing yourself from unwanted lists or email chains. With these strategies, your inbox will be a tool that enhances your productivity, not a source of stress.

Optimize Your Meeting Time

Many things changed in the workplace after COVID-19, including normalizing hybrid and remote work. However, one thing that did not change is the massive number of meetings employees must attend weekly: more than 85% of their time is spent in meetings. The worst part is that half of them are unproductive. The C-suite typically spends around 72% of their time in meetings[1].

For example, since the pandemic, Microsoft research[li] has found that employees saw a 252 percent increase in their weekly meeting time. Similarly, the 2022 Work Trend Index[lii] found that weekly meetings increased by 153 percent.

When employees feel this way, they may start working more outside regular work hours, experience burnout and stress, or simply disengage.

Why are meetings becoming a problem?

- Half of the meetings could be more productive. Around 31 hours are spent on unproductive meetings per month[liii], which cost more than $37 billion annually in salaries.
- Employees complain that meetings are not well organized, derailed by complex questions, dominated by a few employees, or that topics addressed are unimportant to them.
- Employees working in hybrid and remote mode are getting more stressed during meetings due to issues like psychological safety[liv], fear of speaking in public and interacting with a hippo (a leader or high potential).
- Meetings are distractors and drive time fragmentation. Employees need to stop what they are doing and shift their focus to a meeting. The "switching time" reduces employee productivity and interrupts flow. It takes at least 15 minutes to become productive again after a distraction.
- Meetings make you travel, change your schedule or shift priorities.

No-meeting day

Adopting a no-meeting days policy is one way to reduce meetings and time fragmentation. Research published by MIT[lv] surveyed 76 companies, each with over 1,000 employees and operations in more than 50 countries, that had introduced one to five no-meeting days per week (prohibiting even one-on-one meetings) during the past 12 months.

The result was that regardless of the number of meeting-free days instituted, employees reported improved autonomy and cooperation and decreased stress and micromanagement. On the other hand, having too few meetings reduced collaboration and engagement. The best results were achieved at companies with three meeting-free days per week.

When meetings were reduced, productivity increased because employees felt more empowered and autonomous; they had their own to-do lists and held themselves accountable, and satisfaction increased. Employees also decreased the stress of meeting with multiple people and improved collaboration by finding better ways of connecting one-on-one.

How To Significantly Reduce Meetings

Reducing meetings by such a large percentage is not only about moving all the appointments to those days, you can imagine. It is also about being more aware of how much time and energy is wasted and working to improve it.

A great example I always use to see how you can improve time during meetings is using SMED[lvi], a technique that Formula 1 and NASCAR utilize to reduce time spent changing tires. Most people would easily take at least 15 minutes to change one single tire. So, how do Formula 1 cars change all four tires in 2.5 seconds? They understand that time is money and that any extra second counts. Estimate your time in meetings, then estimate your hourly rate and do the math. Of course, you will want to reduce meetings too.

Review the meetings you lead and attend and ask yourself:

- Is this meeting essential to accomplish my goals?
- Can the frequency be reduced or spaced out?
- Are all the attendees actively participating? Do they all need to attend? How can you help them contribute more effectively?
- Can the objective be accomplished through other means, like Slack, mail, or phone calls?
- Can the meeting be reduced to 15 minutes? What about 30 minutes?
- Can you update the company software/app so that your typical meeting timebox is set to be shorter by 15 minutes?
- Can the meeting be replaced with a shorter, more spontaneous 1-on-1 connection?
- Can any tasks be done before or after the meeting to make it shorter but more productive?
- Is the meeting organized enough to accomplish its objective? For example, is an agenda, notetaker, timekeeper or whiteboard needed?
- Do you need other resources/roles to help you make it more effective?
- Do you need to train your team to speak in meetings so that they are more concise or better prepared?
- Ultimately, if in doubt, how would it hurt to try?

While it may sound challenging to reduce meetings at first, inviting everyone to get involved by stating why will gain traction over time. It is no secret that almost every employee complains about meetings. By reducing the company time spent on meetings and improving the productivity of the remaining ones, collaboration and engagement will increase, while stress, anxiety, and burnout will be significantly reduced. Productivity will skyrocket, no doubt.

If you answered yes to any of the questions above, take action. To help you, I would like to share some specific actions you can take to reduce your meeting time by 94% by applying SMED, just like the NASCAR and Formula 1 teams do.

When a meeting is well organized, it can yield a wealth of ideas, energy, and action plans. Meetings are the perfect time to foster a personal connection, share issues promptly and explore suggestions, particularly if you work remotely.

However, you can also get employees' time and attention stuck with no result. Hundreds of unproductive hours a year per employee are lost waiting for other attendees, looking for documents during the meeting, repeating topics, extending discussions without agreeing on a clear action plan, missing key decision-makers or holding attendees that don't participate.

It is your role as a leader to ensure meetings are the most productive part of the day for everyone involved. Your team will develop better ideas, increase engagement, and improve collaboration while you will reduce your meeting time significantly.

SMED stands for single-minute exchange of dies, a method widely used in manufacturing to improve changeover time. In Ford-T times, all cars were black to avoid spending two weeks in changeover time using a different die. Later, Toyota's engineer, Shigeo Shingo, came up with SMED to reduce the process to three minutes.

Experience shows that change over time can dramatically reduce as much as 94%. Formula 1 cars use it to improve tires' changeover time. For many people, changing a single tire can easily take 15 minutes. Changing four tires takes less than 15 seconds for a NASCAR pit crew.

Here are five steps you can follow to SMED your meetings:

Identify a pilot meeting

Choose a periodic meeting that you consider inefficient and focus on improving it first. Don't start with all the sessions simultaneously; choose a team to help improve it.

Identify elements

Dissect all the elements of the meeting: discussions, people talking, voting time, note-taking, waiting time, silence time, idea generation, etc. The most effective way of doing this is to record one of the meetings, have observers take notes, and then work from the recording to create an ordered list of elements. Observers can also identify attendees who are not participating, distracted or multitasking. Estimate also the time lost waiting for the meeting to start, or employees taking over most of the meeting or intimidating others (HIPPO effect), for example.

Identify external tasks

Identify those tasks that could be done at another time, not during the meeting; these are external tasks. External tasks could be done before the meeting, such as retrieving documents, approving previous meeting minutes, getting information, contacting employees who are not present, or preparing the agenda with the topics to discuss. Some tasks that could be done after the meeting are talking about issues in detail, preparing the minutes or checking the status of a report. Most of the time lost during sessions is part of these external elements. While they are in progress, attendees are waiting, and time is lost for everyone, while it could only be spent by one of the team members or eliminated.

Convert Internal Elements to External

This step analyzes the meeting to convert as many internal elements to external as possible. Meetings with several team members, including managers, should be reduced to a minimum number of internal tasks. The rest of the time should be spent individually preparing and reporting the external tasks.

Decision-making or idea generation are usually internal tasks that must be completed during meetings. However, can you prepare these tasks so they can be completed faster? For example, you can define or standardize simple voting methods, routines or decision-making processes in advance.

Many companies hold standup meetings or mini-day 15-minute meetings. The routine is always the same: every employee reports, at the end or beginning of the shift, what is done, what needs to be done today, and what the potential issues are. This routine teaches attendees to be prepared and precise, with a short and sweet speech, being able to share their updates in less than a minute.

Streamline Remaining Elements

The team should ask the following questions for each component: *How can this element be completed in less time? How can we simplify this element?*

For instance, remote teams lose time due to system issues. You could prevent this by ensuring you have the right tools when needed. You can provide information and links in advance so attendees can download the tool, test it and be ready to use it during the meeting.

Teams can complete an SMED project once for each meeting type and then review it regularly as needed. Scrum teams, for example, hold retrospective meetings to review their team process, which is a good time to remember the SMED principles and identify new external tasks.

The beauty of an SMED meeting is that you are not only cutting unproductive meeting time but also better ready to solve issues during the day, reduce redundancy and engage people to communicate more effectively.

Final Thoughts: Doing More With Less

Doing more with less is how to stop this vicious circle of self-pressure. Whether it's maximizing productivity by working fewer hours or finding ways to spend more time doing what you love, finding ways to get more out of what we have can be a valuable skill.

1.   **Start fewer projects and close more.** Being involved in several projects simultaneously reduces our ability to focus. You can channel your energy into finishing tasks and avoid overproducing by simultaneously doing two projects. As a result, you will reduce the projects' lead time and unfinished tasks in the parking lot.

2.   **Multitask less and focus more.** The less time you spend shifting gears, the more you accomplish.

3.   **Spend less time in big group meetings and focus more on your work or doing 1-on-1 sessions.** Spend more time in meetings that will bring you benefits and less on the ones you don't belong to or can't collaborate with.

4.   **Do fewer tasks you don't enjoy and more things you love doing or are good at.** Doing tasks you don't want to drain you. You waste less energy when you want to, and you also get better results. Ask yourself if you can delegate them or do them more quickly or efficiently. Some people may be a better fit for doing those things, while you can be better at doing others. Set aside time for the things that matter most and let go of tasks that aren't as essential. Before accepting a meeting or a task, ask yourself if you are the right person to do the job or if someone else could be a better fit. Saying yes to everything doesn't make you a great coworker but dilutes your boundaries.

5.   **Buy less, use more.** Just as lean methods call for a just-in-time inventory in manufacturing facilities, the same applies in offices and even at home. So much time, money and space are spent on materials you don't get to use, which clutter your space. Reducing, reusing, and recycling are

the three Rs of waste management, which can help keep your space clean and help the environment keep as much material out of the landfill as possible.

6.   Hide less and collaborate more. Collaborating with others can be a great way to get more done with less. By sharing knowledge, resources, and ideas, you can achieve more together than you could on your own.

7.   Overcomplicate less and streamline more. Look for ways to streamline processes and make them more efficient. For example, if you have a to-do list with more than twenty 10-minute tasks, group the functions by category to have fewer items and focus on similar tasks simultaneously. This way, you will reduce shifting time and time spent updating the status of your assignments.

8.   Accept less of the status quo and create more. Look for creative solutions to problems and challenges. Sometimes, doing more with less requires thinking unconventionally and finding unconventional ways to achieve your goals.

9.   Stress less and thank more. Stress and burnout often start with people getting anxious about the future or depressed about past experiences. Unfortunately, you cannot change the past or predict the future. You can only remind yourself where you are right now, be thankful for what you have, and focus on what is possible. While it is hard to manage negative thoughts, you can always try to replace them with positive ones. When negative self-talk kicks in, have positive thoughts on your phone or a booklet to talk to yourself positively.

10.   Focus less on results and more on progress. Our society's extreme focus on results is detrimental to mental health. Instead, focus more on what you can control and your progress daily. Spend less time finding while unrealistic goals are not met, find ways to support the progress, and define robust systems.

By doing more with less, you can save time, money, and other resources, be more productive and enjoy the process.

Acknowledgments

I would like to express my heartfelt gratitude to my family, especially my husband, Guillermo Maiale, whose unwavering support has been a constant source of strength. To my daughters, Sol and Sofia, thank you for your love, joy, and patience. And thanks to my brother Alexis for his support and inspiration.

A special thank you goes to my coachees and mentors, whose insights, courage and guidance have shaped my understanding of time management and the power of compassion. Your encouragement and wisdom continue to inspire me every day.

I am also profoundly grateful to my colleagues who took the time to review this book before its launch, especially Mariana Maeda, Matias Breccia, Luigi Sille, Lauren Hartel and Nikki Wood. Your thoughtful feedback and suggestions have helped refine and elevate this work, and I couldn't have done it without your support.

This book is a testament to all of you—thank you for being an integral part of my journey.

Recommended Tools

Sunsama: A Partner in Your Timeboxing Journey

In this book, we've explored timeboxing as a powerful strategy to enhance productivity and well-being. But for timeboxing to truly work, you need a tool that supports your goals, keeps you organized, and helps you implement these strategies seamlessly into your daily life.

That's where Sunsama comes in.

Sunsama is the perfect platform to implement the timeboxing strategies shared in this book. With its intuitive daily planning tools, Sunsama allows you to break down your most important tasks into time-blocked sections, helping you focus on one thing at a time and make real progress on your goals.

Here's how you can use Sunsama to implement timeboxing effectively:

Plan Your Day with Purpose: Start each day by breaking down your to-dos into specific, timeboxed slots. Sunsama's interface encourages you to be intentional about how you spend your time through guided planning. You can prioritize your "Do Now" (your most important tasks), so you can focus on what matters most.

Maintain Focus: By using the "focus mode" feature, you can set dedicated focus periods for your tasks and avoid distractions. This structure helps prevent the overwhelm of multitasking and keeps you in a productive flow.

Unified daily view: Pull in tasks from Trello/Asana/etc, emails from Gmail/Outlook or meetings from all your calendars in one place.

Realistic Daily Goals: You can decide in advance how long you want to work on each task and set an in-app timer

Track Your Progress: Sunsama's tracking features let you visualize how much time you've dedicated to each task each day, helping you evaluate if you're on track to meet your goals by the end of the week. You can celebrate progress, big or small, and adjust your approach if necessary. You will receive an automatic AI message with your daily highlights, summarizing what you have accomplished daily.

Try Sunsama Free for 1 Month!

Bring the TIMEBOX method to life with Sunsama—your all-in-one tool to stay focused, organized, and in control of your time.

Claim your free trial:
www.sunsama.com/a/timebox

Want to Go Deeper?

Your journey doesn't end here. To help you put these strategies into action, I've created free companion resources, including:

🌎 **Time Management Personality Quiz** – Discover your unique time style so you can personalize your plan.

🎦 **Timebox On-Demand Course** – Master the method at your own pace with videos and downloadable templates.

📝 **Printable Worksheets, Checklists and Downloadables** – Tools to support your daily timeboxing practice.

💬 **1-on-1 Coaching Sessions** – If you want personalized guidance, book a coaching session to move forward with clarity and confidence.

All are available at:
www.lucypaulise.com/timebox

Notes and References

i https://www.forbes.com/sites/lucianapaulise/2023/06/14/reduce-these-8-hidden-wastes-to-stay-productive-not-overwhelmed/?sh=2a0162912626

ii www.sunsama.com/a/timebox

iii Luciana Paulise, "How to Boost Productivity and Wellbeing with 10-Minute Exercise Snacks," *Forbes*, February 25, 2025, **https://www.forbes.com/sites/lucianapaulise/2025/02/25/how-to-boost-productivity-and-wellbeing-with-10-minute-exercise-snacks/**.

iv "Mindfulness and Fitness," *Google Store*, accessed March 6, 2025, **https://store.google.com/intl/en/ideas/articles/mindfulness-and-fitness/**.

v Mark, Gloria, Daniela Gudith, and Ulrich Klocke. "The Cost of Interrupted Work: More Speed and Stress." In *Proceedings of the 26th Annual CHI Conference on Human Factors in Computing Systems*, 107-110. 2008. https://doi.org/10.1145/1357054.1357072.

vi Luciana Paulise, "Mastering Focus: 3 Tips to Improve Your Productivity & Time," *Forbes*, August 21, 2023, **https://www.forbes.com/sites/lucianapaulise/2023/08/21/mastering-focus-3-tips-to-improve-your-productivity-time/?sh=25b3ec571436**.

vii Covey, Stephen R. *The 7 Habits of Highly Effective People: Powerful Lessons in Personal Change*. New York: Free Press, 1989.

viii Sharon Martin, *The CBT Workbook for Perfectionism: Evidence-Based Skills to Help You Let Go of Self-Criticism, Build Self-Esteem & Find Balance* (Oakland, CA: New Harbinger Publications, 2019).

ix Michael Chui et al., THE SOCIAL ECONOMY: UNLOCKING VALUE AND PRODUCTIVITY THROUGH SOCIAL TECHNOLOGIES, McKinsey Global Institute, July 2012, https://www.mckinsey.com/industries/technology-media-and-telecommunications/our-insights/the-social-economy

x "Duration, Batching, and Self-Interruption: Patterns of Email Use on Productivity and Stress." *Academia.edu*, n.d. **https://www.academia.edu/67979293/D_uration_Batching_and_S_elf_interruption_Patterns_of_E_mail_U_se_on_P_roductivity_and_S_tress**.

xi Kostadin Kushlev and Elizabeth W. Dunn, "Checking Email Less Frequently Reduces Stress," *Computers in Human Behavior* 43

(February   2015):   220-228,
https://doi.org/10.1016/j.chb.2014.10.042.

xii Klaus Moser, "Coping with Information Overload in Email Communication: Evaluation of a Training Intervention," *Academia.edu*, accessed [date you accessed the article], **https://www.academia.edu/17416975/Coping_with_inform ation_overload_in_email_communication_Evaluation_of _a_training_intervention.**

xiii Luciana Paulise, "Here Is Why Batching Emails Beats Continuous Checking," *Forbes*, August 13, 2024, **https://www.forbes.com/sites/lucianapaulise/2024/08/13/ here-is-why-batching-emails-beats-continuous-checking/.**

xiv Tim Ferriss, *The 4-Hour Workweek: Escape 9-5, Live Anywhere, and Join the New Rich* (New York: Crown Publishing Group, 2007)

xv Gloria Mark, Daniela Gudith, and Ulrich Klocke, "Duration, Batching, and Self-Interruption: Patterns of E-Mail Use on Productivity and Stress," *Academia.edu*, **https://www.academia.edu/67979293/D_uration_Batchin g_and_S_elf_interruption_Patterns_of_E_mail_U_se_on _P_roductivity_and_S_tress?email_work_card=thumbnai l.**

xvi Luciana Paulise, "10 Tips to Accomplish More with Less in 2023," *Forbes*, January 10, 2023, **https://www.forbes.com/sites/lucianapaulise/2023/01/10/ 10-tips-to-accomplish-more-with-less-in-2023/.**

xvii National Institute of Mental Health. "Attention-Deficit/Hyperactivity Disorder (ADHD)." *National Institute of Mental Health.* Last modified February 2023. **https://www.nimh.nih.gov/health/topics/attention-deficit-hyperactivity-disorder-adhd.**

xviii

https://www.forbes.com/sites/lucianapaulise/2022/11/22/5-steps-to-increase-engagement-at-work-by-achieving-flow-state/?sh=7d4b4eeb5874

xix Csikszentmihalyi, Mihaly. *Flow: The Psychology of Optimal Experience.* New York: Harper & Row, 1990.

xx Héctor García and Francesc Miralles, *Ikigai: The Japanese Secret to a Long and Happy Life* (London: Penguin Life, 2017).

xxi Rafael Nadal, *Rafa: My Story* (New York: Atria Books, 2011).

xxii Ethan Kross, *Chatter: The Voice in Our Head, Why It Matters, and How to Harness It* (New York: Riverhead Books, 2021).

[xxiii] Amy Cuddy, "Your Body Language May Shape Who You Are," TED, June 2012, video, 21:02, https://www.ted.com/talks/amy_cuddy_your_body_langu age_may_shape_who_you_are

[xxiv] Luciana Paulise, *5S Your Life: Stop procrastination and start self-organization* (Beaumont, self-published, 2020).

[xxv] Richard Boyatzis, Melvin Smith, and Ellen Van Oosten, *Helping People Change: Coaching with Compassion for Lifelong Learning and Growth* (Boston: Harvard Business Review Press, 2019).

[xxvi] Jha, Amishi. "The Mindfulness of Breathing: Exercise with Neuroscientist Amishi Jha." *Mindful*, accessed January 29, 2025. https://www.mindful.org/the-mindfulness-of-breathing-exercise-with-neuroscientist-amishi-jha/

[xxvii] Attention Deficit Disorder Association, "ADHD Workplace Accommodations Guide," *ADD.org*, accessed January 13, 2025, https://add.org/adhd-workplace-accommodations-guide/.

[xxviii] Luciana Paulise, *5S Your Life: Stop procrastination and start self-organization* (Beaumont, self-published, 2020).

[xxix] Stephen Denning, *The Age of Agile: How Smart Companies Are Transforming the Way Work Gets Done* (New York: AMACOM, 2018).

[xxx] Richard C. Schwartz, *Internal Family Systems Therapy*, 2nd ed. (New York: Guilford Press, 2019).

[xxxi] Ken Royal, "Who's Responsible for Employee Engagement?" GALLUP, October 28, 2019, https://www.gallup.com/workplace/266822/engaged-employees-differently.aspx.

[xxxii] Sharon Martin, *The CBT Workbook for Perfectionism: Evidence-Based Skills to Help You Let Go of Self-Criticism, Build Self-Esteem & Find Balance* (Oakland, CA: New Harbinger Publications, 2019).

[xxxiii] Carol S. Dweck, *Mindset: The New Psychology of Success* (New York: Random House, 2006).

[xxxiv] Clance, P. R., & Imes, S. A. (1978). The Impostor Phenomenon in High Achieving Women: Dynamics and Therapeutic Intervention. *Psychotherapy: Theory, Research & Practice*, 15(3), 241–247.

[xxxv] Martin E. P. Seligman, *Flourish: A Visionary New Understanding of Happiness and wellbeing* (New York: Atria Books, 2011).

[xxxvi] Kristin Neff, *Self-Compassion: The Proven Power of Being Kind to Yourself* (New York: William Morrow, 2011),

xxxvii Ann Pietrangelo, "Self-Compassion: Benefits, Examples, & Tips," *Medical News Today*, November 8, 2017, https://www.medicalnewsttoday.com/articles/321024.php.

xxxviii Irons, Chris, and Elaine Beaumont. *The Compassionate Mind Workbook: A Step-by-Step Guide to Developing Your Compassionate Self.* Robinson, 2010.

xxxix Diana Hill, "Why Non-Attachment May Be Key to Your Success," *Psychology Today*, March 23, 2022, **https://www.psychologytoday.com/us/blog/striving-thriving/202203/why-non-attachment-may-be-key-your-success?amp.**

xl American Psychological Association. *Compounding Pressure: The Additional Burdens of Stress on Workers in Underserved Populations.* 2021. **https://www.apa.org/pubs/reports/work-wellbeing/compounding-pressure-2021.**

xli "How to Recover from Work Stress, According to Science." *Harvard Business Review*, July 2022. **https://hbr.org/2022/07/how-to-recover-from-work-stress-according-to-science.**

xlii Rutledge, Pamela B. "Why Writing by Hand Is Better for Your Brain." *Psychology Today*, March 7, 2024. **https://www.psychologytoday.com/us/blog/positively-media/202403/writing-by-hand-can-boost-brain-connectivity.**

xliii Paulise, Luciana. "Empower Your Mind: 5 Ways to Take Control of Your Negative Self-Talk." *Forbes*, June 15, 2023. **https://www.forbes.com/sites/lucianapaulise/2023/06/15/empower-your-mind-5-ways-to-take-control-of-your-negative-self-talk/?sh=51de9a13cae9.**

xliv Luciana Paulise, "The 2022 Status of Remote Work and Top Future Predictions," *Forbes*, December 8, 2022, **https://www.forbes.com/sites/lucianapaulise/2022/12/08/the-2022-status-of-remote-work-and-top-future-predictions/?sh=536647351310.**

xlv Luciana Paulise, "4 Reasons to Start Adopting the 3-Meeting-Free Days Policy," https://www.lucypaulise.com/blog/3-meeting-free-days-policy.

xlvi Gallup. "Employee Burnout: Causes and Cures." Gallup, November 9, 2021. **https://www.gallup.com/workplace/508898/employee-burnout-causes-cures.aspx**

xlvii Hinojosa, José A., Inmaculada A. García, Javier García, and José A. García. "Cognitive Flexibility and Its Influence on Emotional Regulation in a Clinical Sample." *Frontiers in Psychology* 6 (2015): 670. **https://www.frontiersin.org/articles/10.3389/fpsyg.2015.0 0670/full**

xlviii Boyatzis, Richard, Melvin Smith, and Ellen Van Oosten. *Helping People Change: Coaching with Compassion for Lifelong Learning and Growth.* Boston: Harvard Business Review Press, 2019.

xlix https://try.sanebox.com/timeboxing

l Luciana Paulise, "The 30-Minutes Challenge—How to Reduce Your Meeting Time," FORBES, June 16, 2020, **https://www.forbes.com/sites/lucianapaulise/2020/06/16/ the-30-minutes-challengehow-to-reduce-your-meeting-time/.**

li Paulise, Luciana. "The 2022 Status of Remote Work and Top Future Predictions." *Forbes*, December 8, 2022. **https://www.forbes.com/sites/lucianapaulise/2022/12/08/ the-2022-status-of-remote-work-and-top-future-predictions/?sh=536647351310.**

lii Microsoft. "Great Expectations: Making Hybrid Work Work." *Microsoft WorkLab.* Accessed January 20, 2025. **https://www.microsoft.com/en-us/worklab/work-trend-index/great-expectations-making-hybrid-work-work.**

liii Atlassian. "The Cost of Time Wasting at Work [Infographic]." *Atlassian*, last modified November 12, 2021. **https://www.atlassian.com/time-wasting-at-work-infographic.**

liv Luciana Paulise, "How to Increase Psychological Safety in a Virtual Team," *Forbes*, September 8, 2020, **https://www.forbes.com/sites/lucianapaulise/2020/09/08 /how-to-increase-psychological-safety-in-a-virtual-team/?sh=414e1c0e1abd.**

lv Tung, Li. "The Surprising Impact of Meeting-Free Days." *MIT Sloan Management Review*, December 22, 2022. **https://sloanreview.mit.edu/article/The-Surprising-Impact-of-Meeting-Free-Days/?utm_source=newsletter&utm_medium=email&utm _content=The%20Surprising%20Impact%20of%20Meeting-Free%20Days&utm_campaign=Best%20of%202022%20En ews%2012/22/2022.**

[lvi] Luciana Paulise, "5 Steps to Help Improve Your Meeting Time and Productivity," *Forbes*, September 28, 2020, https://www.forbes.com/sites/lucianapaulise/2020/09/28/5-steps-to-help-improve-your-meeting-time-and-productivity/?sh=be3c1027a20c.